MONSIEUR
VINCENT

MONSIEUR VINCENT

The Story of St. Vincent de Paul

By HENRI DANIEL-ROPS

Translated from the French
by Julie Kernan

Illustrated with photographs
and line drawings

HAWTHORN BOOKS, INC.
Publishers · New York 11

FIRST EDITION

April, 1961

NIHIL OBSTAT   IMPRIMATUR
Joseph H. Brady, S.T.D.   Thomas A. Boland, S.T.D.
    CENSOR LIBRORUM   ARCHBISHOP OF NEWARK

                        March 14, 1961

The Nihil obstat and Imprimatur are a declaration that a book or pamphlet is
considered to be free from doctrinal or moral error. It is not implied that those who
have granted the Nihil obstat and Imprimatur agree with the contents, opinions
or statements expressed.

Contents

List of Illustrations

These follow page 101

Monsieur Vincent

Monsieur Vincent knew
all those
whom Paris had gathered
inside its walls:
rich and poor,
gentlemen of the Court
and ladies in their carriages,
adventurers of cloak and dagger,
but also the little people
on the banks of the Seine—
the sick, the crippled, beggars,
men condemned to the galleys . . .
Here they are,
assembled in these margins
to illuminate
the eternal features
of a man
and a saint.

Monsieur Vincent

On September 27, 1660, an old man died in the Parisian priory of Saint-Lazare, for nearly thirty years past the motherhouse of the "Priests of the Mission." He was surrounded by affection so unanimous that the whole city looked upon his death as a tragedy.

During the weeks this man in his eighties awaited the Lord's summons, how many messages had come for him! The great and the powerful, the lowly and the humble, all were among the anxious visitors who had stood at the porter's gate waiting for news. The Pope himself had dispatched blessing to this beloved son. From far-off Africa a poor Negro had sent medicinal plants with the assurance that they would ease all suffering. In the churches of Paris hundreds of Masses had been requested to implore heaven for his recovery.

The old man, however, had watched the coming

of his final hour with the peaceful courage and joyful serenity that marked his whole life. So long as he was able to remain on his feet he had continued to go about directing the great works he had founded. For several months he had been unable to walk and had had himself carried to his posts of duty, not without making—for his sense of irony was still lively—the little mocking remark: "Now I am a great lord, the equal of bishops!"

No suffering had wrested a complaint from him, neither had any of the barbarous methods of treatment used by the quack doctors who claimed to be able to cure the abscess on his eye. Over and over he said to those about him: "Let us give ourselves to God, my children, and may He give us the grace to hold fast!"

It was while repeating this great counsel that he surrendered his soul to Him he had served with all his strength. And among those who witnessed his noble death some repeated the consoling words of

St. John of the Cross: "Lord, even though you slay me, it is to change death into life."

The news of his death had scarcely become known when Saint-Lazare was besieged by crowds from every quarter. Those bearing France's greatest names mixed with the people of the slums to file for hour after hour before the narrow pallet where his body rested. The day of his funeral the church of Saint-Germain-l'Auxerrois was much too small to hold those who came to hear his eulogy from the lips of the bishop of Puy, Henri de Maupas. And already from a hundred parts of Christendom, from Rome itself, came messages asking for the favor of some relics. . . .

This aged man canonized by the voice of the Christian people, this dead man surrounded by affection so universal, was a priest, a simple priest who never in his life had wished to be anything else. His name was Vincent de Paul. Far and wide he was known as *Monsieur Vincent*.

The lessons of life

"Oh, what treasures are hidden in Holy Providence, and what sovereign honor they render to Our Lord who follow Providence and do not encroach on it." When he wrote these words to his friend Louise de Marillac, around the year 1629, was Monsieur Vincent thinking of his personal experience? He himself had been late in discovering the treasures hidden in Holy Providence and truly he had never "encroached on it." Providence had always sufficed him, and even when he did not know it, it was leading him on his way and he allowed it to guide him.

It was indeed necessary for Providence to take a hand with this son of a humble peasant of the Landes—a grubby lad who, at the age of six, led the pigs to feed on acorns—to transform him into 14 the most honored churchman of his times and even more: one of the most complete saints, the most effectual of all time. To tell the truth, Providence was in no hurry. The Lord allowed this man to go through the most varied experiences, knowing that for the task that faced him none of these experiences would be useless.

So it was that he who was to become the apostle of the humblest laboring people was born of the poorest of France's poor. His name, traditionally written in a way that denotes nobility, should not deceive us. The Depauls were not noble themselves nor were they connected with the nobility. They were always very modest people, working a soil that was not rich, and they had little to eat from one year's end to the other save the millet boiled in a pot from which each filled his bowl.

On the border between the region of the Landes and the richer Chalosse country, but situated on the less desirable side among sands and marshlands, Pouy, at the end of the sixteenth century, was only a group of mud huts with thatched roofs. The town of Dax—it was then called Acqs—was far away, more than seven miles distant. No highway led in or out of Pouy. France then had hundreds of such villages where the support of a family of six children meant back-breaking labor.

It was at Ranquines on the outskirts of Pouy— known today and since 1828 as Saint-Vincent-de-Paul—that little Vincent was born, probably in 1580. We say probably because the real date is not exactly known. The saint's first biographer, Abelly, puts it as April 24, 1576, but there are reasons to believe this good bishop put down the date incorrectly for pious reasons, so as to be able to say that in the year 1600, when Vincent was ordained, he had reached the canonical age of twenty-four. When, in 1639, Vincent de Paul testified at the trial of Saint-Cyran, he himself declared that he was fifty-nine years old; and again in his deposition during the process of beatification of St. Francis de Sales, he gave an age that confirmed the same date. Whether it was 1576 or 1580 or, as his later biographer, Père Coste, has it, 1581, and apart from the question of his precise age at the time of ordination, none of this was seriously to affect the future of this child.

What is certain is that very early Vincent, the third son of de Paul, a peasant, and of his wife, Bertrande de Moras, was a precocious child whose intelligence shone from his eyes and whose witty speech amused the country people. He was noticed by Monsieur de Comet, a notable of Dax who came regularly to Pouy to fulfill his functions as "magistrate of the parish," and who offered to help the boy with his education. At that time the only career promising advancement for so poor a boy was the Church. So Vincent spent nine years at Dax studying with the Franciscans. Admirably receptive, knowing how to learn and quick to understand, even more attentive to life's experiences, he happily followed the courses of study, a brilliant student. At fifteen, minor orders were conferred on him and he received the tonsure. For overcoming social barriers, nothing could compare with the priesthood.

And such it seems was his sole intention: to become a priest in order to escape from the mud of his native village. This childhood ambition was not without its dangers, for he was later to confess to the temptations of pride it brought him: "I remember once at the college," he wrote, "when I was a student someone came to tell me that my father, a poor peasant, was asking for me. I refused to go to speak to him, and here I committed a great sin."

That he had great contrition for it no one can doubt, for later, when he became powerful at Court and flunkeys bent before him, he never lost an occasion to recall his very modest origins and to speak of himself as the son of a humble woman "who never had a servant, and who had been in service herself." He even succeeded somewhat in deceiving posterity about himself and for a long time passed as what he hardly was: "the simple, good man," as Bremond says, "the shrewd peasant, the tottering old beggar friar that we have had represented to us."

However that may be, Depaul, Vincent's worthy father, did not hold the incident against him. When Vincent's studies with the Franciscans were completed and it was a question of him going to the University, the good man made a heroic gesture. To pay the expenses of his son's studies, he sold a pair of oxen. . . .

Vincent was thus enabled to follow courses under the masters at Toulouse. He himself gave lessons, even sold soup to his more affluent fellow students, to eke out his living. In this way he arrived at the age of twenty.

On September 23, 1600, Vincent paid a visit to the blind old bishop of Périgueux, François de Bourdeilles. Overwhelming the old man with solicitude, Vincent asked for ordination. The bishop immediately granted his request; that was the way of the times.

However, his studies were not yet finished; they had to be continued four more years before the University would grant the "letters of attestation" conferring on him the degree of bachelor of theology. But Vincent was a priest, and before long he had the university title. There remained but to find a means to embark on his career, namely to secure a benefice, or living—some choice parish, some canon's stall. In this matter he busied himself actively, as he himself recounts, being, as he expressed it, "caught up in the web of the spider."

To carry out its designs for this little priest in quest of prebend, Providence had recourse to singular means. These means were so curious, indeed, that certain distrustful historians have placed them in doubt and qualified as a vast tissue of inventions the account Vincent gave of what happened. It is difficult, however, to imagine that a saint would lie knowingly, or that at least he would not later disavow tales made up in his youth, if such were merely tales. . . . It may be better to accept as truth the contents of two letters which Vincent addressed on July 24, 1607 and February 28, 1608, to his protector, Monsieur de Comet, telling him about his adventure.

A good woman of Toulouse left Vincent a sizeable inheritance, and he had to go to Marseilles to collect it—for the legacy had first to be recovered from a "villainous rogue" who had made off with the woman's assets. In returning, Vincent had the unfortunate idea of taking the route by sea, and embarked on a ship leaving for Narbonne. The weather was fine, the voyage began auspiciously. Alas, pirates were on the prowl, and three Barbary brigantines appeared on the horizon. The peaceful ship was stopped and boarded. Crew and passengers were captured, and Vincent found himself a slave in Algeria, sold in the marketplace like a bull at a fair.

Nevertheless, the Lord had not abandoned him in this trial. After a brief period spent on a fishing boat, where seasickness made him unfit for any work, he was resold to a "spagyric doctor"—we might call him a pharmacist or chemist—a transmuter of metals who spent his time seeking the philosopher's stone. This man, in turn, sold Vincent to a planter, a Savoyard from Nici (Annecy), a former monk who had become an apostate. The impression Vincent made on this man was considerable. It was perhaps even more upon the three

women who made up the harem of the ex-friar.

Remembering his own role as a priest, Vincent reminded his master of his duties and in a way so persuasive that the man was brought back to God. And one day, the master and the slave embarked together, secretly, for France.

Monsieur Vincent's ecclesiastical career began with this unexpected twist. Disembarking at Aigues-Mortes, at the end of June 1607, the two fugitives went to Avignon where the Vice-Legate, Pierre Montorio, received them with "tears in his eyes and a sob in his throat," happy to welcome back into the fold of the Church the repentant renegade and to shower suitable honors on the heroic priest who had visibly acted in the affair as God's instrument. The public ceremony edified the spectators enormously.

Perhaps this is the place to stress the evident gift we must recognize in Monsieur Vincent: the faculty of attracting and persuading all those he approached, whether they were magistrates of Toulouse, such as Monsieur de Comet, "spagyric" doctors, African planters, or bishops such as Monseigneur de Bourdeilles or Pierre Montorio. Thenceforth, under the charm of the young priest, Vice-Legate Montorio proposed that Vincent accompany him on a trip he must make to Rome: he was loath to separate himself from the beguiling talker who had such fascinating things to tell and who brought back from Barbary so many of

the secrets of alchemy—a science that secretly intrigued the Pope's representative.

It was therefore in Rome that Vincent de Paul finished his studies. He did more: he learned to know the personages of the Pontifical Court and this knowledge would one day become most useful to him. But after eighteen months the experience seemed to him sufficient. As he wrote to Monsieur de Comet, he hoped to obtain through the affection and benevolence of the Vice-Legate "the means of making an honorable retirement" by obtaining a good benefice in France. For this purpose, would they send him from Acqs a copy of his letters of ordination duly signed and sealed by the bishop?

This was done, and Vice-Legate Montorio went so far in his benevolence as to recommend his young friend to the French Ambassador, Count Savary de Brève, who like everyone else was conquered by Vincent de Paul's graces. So, in 1609, Vincent arrived in Paris, certainly the bearer of letters from the ambassador, and perhaps invested with a secret mission. Of the nature of this we know nothing except that it led to an audience with Henry IV who, being a Bearnais, was charmed by his near-compatriot.

A short time later, de Paul, son of peasants was appointed chaplain to Queen Margaret of Navarre, ex-wife of the "Vert Galant." Soon he held a benefice—the living of Saint-Léonard-des-Chaumes, a Cistercian abbey in the diocese of Saintes—a comfortable life. But had Providence taken so much trouble to achieve just this result?

For those God singles out, everything is useful, even those things apparently farthest from Him. Concern for advancement—legitimate in a way but nothing which has ever led anyone to sanctity—placed Vincent de Paul precisely in situations where accidental meetings became decisive and were to bring him out of his "little periphery" to place him at the very heart of his vocation.

Was it only by accident that the hospital of the Brothers of St. John of God faced the mansion of Queen Margaret, so that Monsieur Vincent might visit the sick and serve his apprenticeship in the misery and suffering of the destitute? Was it only by accident that among all the fine people to whom he had access, an exceptional man—Cardinal de Bérulle—held high place?

At no time given to personal confidences, Monsieur Vincent was never to explain the evolution by which a little priest with temporal ambitions was changed into an apostle destined for the honors of the altar. Was there a fiery night such as Pascal describes? A slow transformation? Who can say?

It is, however, certain that Cardinal Bérulle played a part and had great influence in the birth of this new man. Bérulle, the first master of the French school of spirituality dear to Henri Bremond; Bérulle, the founder of the Oratorian Fathers, the first in date of the great reformers of the French clergy. A tradition, unfortunately unsupported by any document, has it that in 1611 Vincent made a retreat with Bérulle and also with the spiritually solid Adrien Bourdoise, who, in his parish of Saint-Nicolas-du Chardonnet, was at that time carrying on a curious experiment in clerical community living.

Nevertheless, it is certain that henceforth Bérulle's influence on Monsieur Vincent's career was constant. It was upon his proposal that the worldly chaplain of the ex-queen Margaret of Navarre consented to become the curé of a parish. This was in no sense a promotion, since it was a country parish of market gardeners and humble laborers at Clichy-La Garenne.

In this new task, Vincent succeeded beyond all expectations. His words, his constant and devoted watchfulness, his gift for organizing, which became immediately evident, all contributed to success with his humble flock. When the Archbishop of Paris made a pastoral visit and asked the curé how he felt about his work, he received this reply: "I am more content than I can say. . . . My people are so good and obedient in regard to all the things I recommend to them, that I say to myself: neither the Pope nor you could be happier than I am!"

It is understandable that Cardinal de Bérulle was impressed by this success, but why at the end of a year, did he bring to a halt Vincent's work as pastor of Clichy? Probably it was because this good judge of men had decided that for Vincent a country parish was too small a stage; he should be enabled to play a more important role.

At exactly that time a distinguished family asked the founder of the Oratory to find a tutor for its boys. The Gondis were excellent Christians, even more—souls aspiring to sanctity. Moreover, Count de Gondi, General of the Galleys, might become a useful protector to assist Vincent de Paul to go one step farther. And so it turned out.

Again we must admire the quality Vincent de Paul had to charm hearts and conquer souls. In these surroundings, new to him, among personages high in noble rank and financial affairs, he not only succeeded; he became literally indispensable. Soon it was not only the Gondi sons whom he guided but also the mother, an excellent character full of good will and the desire to do good, and the father. His ascendancy over the latter became so great that on one occasion Vincent even prevented him from fighting a duel.

How did he win him over? Vincent has himself explained his method, and the least we can say of this method is that it was astonishing. "I had as a maxim," he wrote, "to consider the General of the Galleys as God, and God as him, and to obey him in the same way, and to obey Madame as I would the Blessed Virgin. . . ." We may surmise that this humility and obedience went hand in hand with tact, goodness and generosity, and also with firmness. All, including the servants in the Gondi house, surrounded the tutor with obvious veneration.

Again a success, a step forward in a fine career. Yet suddenly, at one stroke, Monsieur Vincent brought it to an end.

The next episode in the life of Vincent is seen by

the biographers of the saint as the one in which his vocation finally became defined: his departure for Châtillon.

One recalls the attempted flights of the Curé of Ars, when Jean-Baptiste Marie Vianney abandoned his parish, considering himself unworthy to carry on the pastoral ministry. Was it a similar feeling of unworthiness that at this time moved Monsieur Vincent? Or was it an imperious, exacting call from God to other tasks than educating two boys, even though at the same time he directed their noble parents? At this point can be perceived, under the apparently calm and smiling appearance of this saint, one of those pathetic self-debates in which every man must face himself and measure alone what God expects of him.

Once more Bérulle profoundly understood. When he received from his protégé a letter saying that he felt "interiorly pressed by God to go to some distant province to spend his whole life in teaching and serving the poor people of the countryside," the understanding Cardinal accepted this. At this moment he was able to produce a very woebegone parish, lost in the midst of the marshes: Châtillon-des-Dombes. He allowed Monsieur Vincent to quit the manor of the Gondis to become a peasant curé.

As a matter of fact, one of Vincent's reasons for attempting this adventure grew out of an experience he had, in January 1617, in company with Madame de Gondi. Accompanying her on a visit to one of her domains in Picardy, he had been asked

by her to preach to the peasants. What he had seen in that canton of Folleville, not far from Amiens, had wrung his heart: the spiritual poverty of the rural masses was widespread and yet the good will of these souls was certain. Why did the Church wait to till these fields? Doubtless the son of the peasants of the Landes dreamed of missions to bring Christ again to the backwoods poor of France. . . . And on the road he now saw before him Châtillon-des-Dombes was a step forward.

The faithful of Châtillon were never to forget the first months' work of their amazing pastor. He had been received at first with a certain distrust, this curé who arrived from Paris and spoke with a curious sing-song accent. In but a few days he had made his impact. For this priest but little resembled the others, notably the half-dozen "chaplains" who up to that time had given so little care to souls.

He was seen repairing and cleaning his church with his own hands; the people remarked that his sermons were well worth listening to, and that his liturgical services were not at all boring. They saw him praying hour after hour . . . rising before dawn, he celebrated Mass daily, which at that period was exceptional.

In several weeks the village was transformed: the chaplains came to lodge at the rectory with the new pastor; nothing reprehensible went on in the bell-tower whereas formerly, it was said, the gatherings held were far from exemplary. Even the Huguenot nobleman Jean Beynier, who had consented to receive Monsieur Vincent in his home, had been so won over that he was said to be on the road to conversion. A fresh wind blew over the entire countryside.

One Sunday, just as the pastor was about to mount the pulpit, a parishioner came up and whispered something to him. Over Monsieur Vincent's expressive face passed a shadow. And when he spoke, his words deeply moved the entire congregation. He did not make moralizing comments, but a precise, concrete and heart-breaking statement of fact: on the outskirts of the parish, far from the village and in the midst of the marshes, a whole family was perishing of sickness, hunger, isolation and distress. The pastor's appeal was heard. One must not allow one's brother to perish! And that afternoon some fifty good people set out on the road with baskets on their arms, carrying help to the abandoned.

The power of charity! But there was more to it than that. Vincent was not only an emotional and sensitive man, moved to the depth of his being by pity; he was not merely an orator—to tell the truth he could hardly be called an orator at all. Able to move audiences deeply, he was a man of action and achievement; an organizer, quick to seize a proffered opportunity and to both cause and transform into practical action the feelings in the hearts of other men and women. In this case he turned those Sunday afternoon visitors into well-disciplined groups in order to carry out their charitable intentions. So was born the *Confraternity of the Ladies of Charity*.

The careful and complete rule Monsieur Vincent drew up immediately for their use was found in 1839 in the municipal archives of Châtillon. We may still see in the church of the village this paper written in the saint's own hand. "The said Confraternity shall be called the Confraternity of Charity in imitation of the Charity in Rome, and those persons of whom it is principally composed shall be called Servants of the Poor or Servants of Charity."

The document should be read in its entirety. Nothing is lacking, not even details of caring for the cleanliness of the sick, nor the menus of the meals to be served them. On December 8, 1617, Vincent was able to announce to his people that the rule of the Confraternity had received the approbation of the vicar general of Lyons (for Châtillon, now belonging to the diocese of Belley, was then a parish of the Lyons diocese). They then proceeded to the election of the directors of the Confraternity. Vincent's first charitable organization sprang, as would all the others, directly from life's lessons.

However, his magnificent experiment at Châtillon did not last. Less than two weeks after the official installation of the Confraternity, a desolate Monsieur Vincent left his beloved flock. Why? The Gondis had not seen their chaplain leave them without feelings of great sorrow. "I am in despair

at a letter Monsieur Vincent has written me," General de Gondi wrote to his wife, and the latter replied in the same vein: "I accuse him of nothing; I must not. But, in truth, his absence is very strange. He knows how much I need his guidance, and the affairs I must discuss with him, the pains of mind and body I have suffered for lack of help, the good I desired to accomplish in my villages and which I find it impossible to undertake without his counsel.... The good he did in my house and for seven or eight thousand souls on our lands is no longer done. Why? Were not these souls redeemed by the precious blood of Our Lord in the same way as those in Bresse? Are they not just as dear to him?"

We may admire in these passages the burning faith that animated souls, the souls of the Gondis as well as Monsieur Vincent's. Such desires, such hopes, were numerous in the bright springtime of that great century of spirituality....

General de Gondi also wrote to his wife in regard to the flight of their beloved chaplain: "In this matter I believe there is no one more powerful than Monsieur de Bérulle...." And, for her part, Madame de Gondi sent Monsieur Vincent a letter in which she declared among other things: "I charge you before God with all those things that I fail to do because of the lack of your help...."

How was it possible to resist such insistence? **30** Monsieur Vincent therefore surrendered. Back in Paris at the beginning of 1618, he created a

"Charity," similar to that at Châtillon, at Ville-preux, a village situated a few miles from Paris on the Gondi lands. Then, journeying through the domains of this powerful family, he created others at Joigny, at Montmiral, and in Folleville.

Several zealous priests attached themselves to him to take up the spiritual work in the French countryside. Vincent de Paul's second great foundation was about to be created. At the same time Monsieur Vincent, now officially chaplain to the Gondis—not only the tutor of their sons and occasional chaplain but also soon to be chaplain general of the Royal Galleys—saw his field of action and his influence growing from day to day.

A last providential encounter still remained to take place before the former ambitious little priest was to be definitely set on the road where God awaited him. This was his meeting with living sanctity. In the course of the year 1618 Monsieur Vincent met the man who at that time embodied saintliness most visibly: St. Francis de Sales. The Bishop of Geneva had come to Paris both to carry out a diplomatic mission and for the purpose of establishing the first French house of the Visitation, the Order he had founded with St. Jeanne de Chantal.

The meeting of these two men, who were equally filled with love of Christ, and the nature of their conversations—sometimes joined in by *31* Jeanne de Chantal, the great foundress—may be guessed from the results. The Bishop of Geneva asked Vincent to become the ecclesiastical superior of the new house, and at his death in 1622, three years later, entrusted this Order to him as well as the spiritual direction of Jeanne de Chantal herself.

This decisive encounter ended one chapter of Monsieur Vincent's life. Did Francis de Sales' "suavity" influence Vincent whose own temper up to that time was quick and sometimes sharp? It was not alone suavity. At the process of beatification of St. Francis de Sales, Vincent declared he had seen Christ Himself when he spoke to the great bishop of Annecy and Geneva. In these encounters he made his discovery of the great law in the Christian advance toward perfection: for all to become like Christ, to make of themselves what

St. Paul described: "It is not I who live, but Christ in me."

Monsieur Vincent drew many things from his conversations with St. Francis de Sales. Beside his teaching of humility, he derived from him an idea, and that was to found a religious order of women who would not be cloistered but would engage in tasks of active charity. This had been St. Francis de Sales' first plan for his Visitation nuns but it had had to be abandoned at the time through the fault of a faint-hearted bishop. Vincent had also seen in Francis the indispensable power of example. Thenceforth Vincent was ready to undertake his great works, ready to be fully the saint that God intended.

Monsieur Vincent the man

Let us now consider Vincent de Paul in what
Dante calls "the middle of the road of life," at the
time of the start of his great achievements, around
the year 1625. His period of training had been
long but rich in varied experiences. He was familiar, directly and personally, with all ranks of society from that of the most humble peasant to the
world of the courtier of Paris and Rome. His
knowledge of men was as immense as his knowledge of the great problems of his times. One is
tempted to believe that it was Providence's supernatural intention for him to pass the age of forty
before he fully found himself.

The best known portrait of Monsieur Vincent,
painted by the meticulous Simon François, is lost
to us today, but it has been popularized by en-
gravings made from it by Van Schuppen and
Edelinck. It was François who created the image

34

—recently made famous by the films—of a small, bearded old man with a strong nose, lined features and a neck sunk into his shoulders. This portrait was painted under difficulties—for, in the case of this model, ruses were necessary—and it is possible Monsieur Vincent did look this way when he was more than seventy. But he had not always been like that.

We can see him in his mature years as a slight, nervous man, quick of gesture and speech, with sparkling eyes nut-brown in color, and thin lips that smiled with gentle irony—a man who charmed everyone on first approach. He was no longer the "young man of Gascony" in clerical garb one had seen in the salon of Queen Margaret; he nevertheless retained the vivacious alertness, the gift of repartee, and the thin sturdiness of his race.

Intelligent? Extraordinarily so, although perhaps not in the sense given the word by intellectuals. His development did not owe a great deal to books, but this is not to say that he was an ignoramus. He possessed to a high degree a gift that is not acquired, of being able to take in at a glance things and beings, to see at once the whole and the minute detail, of perceiving a problem and at the same time its practical solution.

Few minds resemble his in giving such an impression of boundless receptivity. Everything he saw, everything he heard, served for "his advancement"—a word that came many times from his pen and was full of meaning in the sense he used it. And what a realist he was! The very opposite of a visionary, the dreamer of airy dreams, the fabricator of systems. He was Descartes' contemporary, almost a compatriot of Montaigne; one can well understand why he so often said: "Our God asks nothing of us which is contrary to reason."

All this, however, could describe an ambitious man of action, nothing more. But—and to this all his contemporaries testify—a marvelous goodness radiated from his whole being. One does not know if this was spontaneous and natural: goodness is a virtue which is learned and developed like others. However, one fact is certain: at his maturity Monsieur Vincent was entirely good. He loved men; he loved them without any illusions; his mind was lucid; his heart ardent. "He could hear of no human distress without sorrow and compassion showing in his face." This remark of Abelly, his first biographer, is confirmed by a hundred wit-

nesses. He did not love men anonymously, as is too often the case with social theorists. It was not humanity in the abstract that Vincent loved, but a certain being of flesh and blood, miserable and suffering, in whom he recognized a brother. Hence the infinite delicacy to be seen in the least of his actions.

A single example among a hundred: in founding homes for the indigent, he opposed the separation of old couples. To make it possible for them to finish out their lives together he founded the charity called "Little Households," so that the old wife and the old husband might not be separated. This delicate goodness that radiated from his being explains the sort of *aura* that surrounded him. A woman, whose spiritual director he had been, gave this moving testimony: "We may say, as did the disciples on their way to Emmaus: our hearts burned with love of God when Monsieur Vincent spoke to us."

Such are the more apparent reasons for his influence. They explain why the priest in a shabby cassock and raveled sash could gently tease the Queen and still occupy at Court, among the great of the land, the position he did. But we must go beyond these appearances to understand what it was that made Monsieur Vincent even more than a man of good deeds and spiritual influence—what it was that made him a saint.

Henri Bremond gives the perfect answer: "It was not charity that made him a saint, but his

saintliness that made him truly charitable." To put this another way, in Vincent's case we are not dealing with simple human generosity but with Charity itself, in the theological sense of the word, with the Charity of Christ present in all his intentions, all the acts of his life, consecrating and supernaturalizing them.

We must stress this remark in order to clear away certain confusions. Monsieur Vincent's very fame has contributed, as is often the case, to the result of oversimplifying his portrait. And we may add that the film which in recent years has done the most to make him known to the masses has done no little to implant such summary notions. We do not understand Monsieur Vincent's true nature when we see him only as the organizer of soup kitchens, the savior of little children lost in the streets, even—and here we are dealing merely with a legend—as a volunteer galley slave, replacing an unhappy prisoner shackled to the oars. The greatest images of Monsieur Vincent's charity have their real meaning only if this charity is related to God, if we remember that it is only the projection into men's lives of the charity that God has manifested toward them in His Incarnation and His Passion.

And it is not only Monsieur Vincent's charity that bears witness to the ineffable source whence his soul drew the living waters; the same may be said of his other virtues. We receive the impression that these, too, were all acquired by the effort of self over self as he fixed his gaze on a transcendent model. The little boy who refused to go to the parlor to speak to his old peasant father, the little priest in search of prebend, the occupant of the comfortable benefice at Saint-Léonard-des Chaumes—was he humble? Yet the virtue praised most highly by Monsieur Vincent, the virtue he himself tried hardest to practice, the one he never ceased later to preach to his Sons, was the virtue of humility. Why was this, if not that he had been taught by Another that the Kingdom of God has been promised to the humble of heart.

Another virtue he taught and asked of those he directed: simplicity. Did he himself have it by nature? Again Bremond had reason to believe that Monsieur Vincent was naturally a complex being, full of inner contradictions, even perhaps of secret conflicts, "as complex as Fénelon." Here again, was it not Christ who taught him that the first duty of the spiritual man is to achieve interior unity in the Truth that is entire?

Was his prudence, the wisdom recognized in him by all his biographers, his way of "not encroaching on Providence" but at every moment and under every circumstance placing himself in the hands of God with an interior *"fiat voluntas tua"*—was this spontaneous? It hardly seems so, if we judge from his youth. In this respect as in all the others, what developed the human virtues in the soul of St. Vincent and made them so evident in influencing others was his desire to identify himself completely with his Only Model. According to the words of his master Francis de Sales, he wished to be "a perfect follower of Christ"—and all else was added.

The prodigious effectiveness of Monsieur Vincent was, finally, but the very logical and natural result of his intense spiritual life. It must be confessed, however, that this is not the explanation most frequently given for his amazing success. The saint of charity was tremendously active. He was little given to confidences; he guarded jealously what went on in the depths of his soul; and he believed moreover that this was of interest to no one. Going further, he declared on every occasion that he was the last of the ignorant—and those who were inconvenienced by his activities were only too inclined to repeat this declaration. That is one of the reasons so many erroneous ideas were spread about him.

We cannot say it too strongly: in him the man of action can be explained only insofar as he was determined and conditioned by the spiritual man. We understand nothing of his work if we do not recognize in the least of his achievements the intentions of a very great mystic.

A very great mystic—we must define what we mean. St. Vincent de Paul left us no treatises on the mystical life as did St. John of the Cross, or St. Francis de Sales. His spiritual thinking is spread here and there thoughout the *Conferences*

and Conversations he held with his Sons and his Daughters and in the enormous correspondence he kept up throughout his whole life with innumerable people. Collected in a monumental edition by Père Coste, these texts constitute an imposing whole. But there is no use looking through it for a purely theoretical outlook: his teaching sprang from the circumstances and encounters of his life, from difficulties to be surmounted. This does not mean, of course, that his teaching was any the less firm or coherent.

Was his doctrine original? It does not seem so. If it was indeed a doctrine, it was derived from those who helped the saint in his own formation: Bérulle, doubtless, also St. Francis de Sales whose influence is to be found in so many passages of Vincent's writings. But must we disregard the influence of Ignatius of Loyola's *Spiritual Exercises*? Vincent achieved a golden synthesis of these elements. Bérulle's ardent mysticism was combined

41

with the pious humanism of the Bishop of Geneva as with the strict discipline of the Jesuits. Monsieur Vincent had greater confidence in human nature than Bérulle, but he used fewer honeyed words than the author of *The Introduction to the Devout Life*. He was to oppose the error of Jansenism, but it would be impossible to find in him any trace of laxity. On this point, as on many others, he was the precursor of our modern Church. If one had to find some connecting link between him and ourselves, it would be St. Alphonsus Liguori.

Thus the great man of achievement, who rose to exceptional heights in his own day and whose foundations would endure down to our own, also ranks as one of the masters of the great school of spirituality which made France the chosen land of purest mysticism in the first half of the seventeenth century. For Vincent, as for all the masters of this school, the great, the only precept of the spiritual life, the one demanded by "the metaphysics of saints" was the imitation of Christ—or, as Cardinal de Bérulle said, "adherence to Christ." "To desire nothing but what God wills"; to know "He will make use of us if we will give ourselves to Him"; "to empty oneself of self and allow God to act"—such were its commandments, constantly repeated.

We would like to quote two of the most beautiful passages, among his numerous and admirable writings, in which Monsieur Vincent followed and developed such thoughts as these. On May 1, 1635, he wrote to his old friend Father Portail: "Remember often that we live in Jesus Christ through the death of Jesus Christ, and that we must die in Jesus Christ through the life of Jesus Christ; and that our lives should be hidden in Jesus Christ, filled with Jesus Christ; and that in order to die as did Jesus Christ, we must live as did Jesus Christ...."

And twenty years later, in 1656, when sending his advice on the subject of authority to Father Antoine Durand, a Priest of the Mission, he again took up the same theme under another form. How could a good superior acquit himself of the difficult task of leading youthful souls to God? "Certainly, Monsieur, there is nothing human in this; it is not the work of a man, it is God's work. *Grande opus.* It is the continuation of the methods of Jesus Christ. . . . No, Monsieur, neither philosophy, nor theology, nor discourse operate in souls. It is necessary for Jesus to take part with us, for us to work through Him and He through us, for us to speak through Him and in His spirit, as He did in His Father.... Therefore, Monsieur, we must be emptied of ourselves so that we may put on Jesus Christ."

Are we not here at the highest point of mystical experience? We cannot imagine a Carthusian or a Cistercian, a Claretian or a Carmelite lost in contemplation in his cell, speaking in any other language. But the difference between such a man and

43

Monsieur Vincent is that Monsieur Vincent did not wish to pursue the mystical experience by retiring from the world. He wished to be engaged in the world completely, to work among men with every ounce of his strength.

In a lecture given by Monsieur Vincent (appearing in Volume XI of the *Complete Works* collected by Père Coste), we may read this acute analysis of the profound causes for his own attitude: "We must note that love is divided into affective love and effective love. Affective love is a certain flow of the person who loves into the beloved, or the goodness and tenderness one feels for the thing one loves, as the father for his child. Effective love consists in doing those things commanded or desired by the person one loves. And it is of this kind of love I am speaking."

For Monsieur Vincent, affective love and effective love were inseparable. To act for God was to display both these kinds of feeling. It was to bring about in deeds on this mortal earth the wish each day repeated in the Our Father: "Thy Kingdom come"; it was to bring to a still higher level the two loves that make but one. That is why, instead of closing himself within a cloister to be supernaturally effectual through grace and penance and applying the merits he gained to the souls of others, Vincent de Paul, a great mystic, was a mystic of action. Charity, spread through good works, rejoined pure contemplation at the summit. It was on the faces of men that this saint saw and venerated the face of Christ. "The greatest of our men of action," again to quote Bremond, "was given us by mysticism."

Great achievements

This great mystic was, then, a man of action, tireless in his achievements. The thirty-five years of life which Providence granted him after he saw the true road that he must follow until death were filled with accomplishments. Others in his time also did great things: St. Francis de Sales, St. John Eudes, St. Francis Regis, St. Peter Fourier, and the same can be said of those like Bérulle, Louis Lallemant and Olier who have not yet been canonized by the Church.

No other, however, covered so vast a field. In every sort of activity involving the cause of God Monsieur Vincent was to be found at work. Those multiform achievements which we have to enumerate, one after the other, in order to explain them, must be seen as the works of the vigorous hands of a highly spiritual man who was at the same time an organizing genius.

46

Vincent de Paul's name is so bound up with works of charity that we incline to forget that, for him, the great foundations he made in this domain, on the temporal plane, were but secondary. If he never believed that the soul of a man is saved by leaving his body in misery, neither did he forget that for a priest the first duty, the fundamental task, was to save souls. At Folleville in Picardy, at Châtillon in Dombes, what moved him was the neglect of the spiritual needs of the workers of the soil. At Châtillon the very foundation of the Ladies of Charity had as its inspiration an aim spiritual as much as temporal. In banding together to aid those in distress, these women would lift themselves up, would unite themselves to the Christ of Charity, at the same time as they accomplished good works.

Thus the first of his foundations in date—and perhaps absolutely first always in his mind—was a work expressly established for the salvation of

47

souls, expressly instituted to lead them to their immortal destinies: the *Mission*.

"Institutions," "establishments," "foundations": these words, although the historian is constrained to use them, would have caused the saint a kind of horror. Had he ever had the idea—the pretension—of instituting, establishing, founding? If he had, it was without the express intention, allowing himself to be guided by events—for him the voice of divine Providence. To do nothing on his own initiative, but to respond always to the call from above: such was his principle. Under a given circumstance something would take form which, if it pleased God, would endure and throw out solid roots. So it was with all that he brought into being.

In the case of the Missions, Providence assumed in Monsieur Vincent's eyes the human faces of General and Madame de Gondi. In bringing him back from Châtillon with so much effort, these pious people did not intend to monopolize the treasure who was now again under the shelter of their roof. In the moving letter she had written him, Madame de Gondi spoke of the six or seven thousand souls who lived on her land and for whom she felt responsible. She had not forgotten Monsieur Vincent's success, in January 1617, when he had preached to the peasants of Picardy. The seed of a plan had been sown in her mind; she had economized on her clothing and little pleasures, putting aside fifteen thousand livres—a considerable sum for the period—in order to finance regular religious preaching to re-Christianize her people.

Madame Gondi's project took long to put into execution. Two proposals she made to the Oratorians and the Jesuits were declined: those noble companies were not greatly interested in the country people. The idea, therefore, came to her to institute a new society of which the superior would be no other than her chaplain, her beloved spiritual director. The idea was approved by General de Gondi with such warmth that he tripled the initial capital. With forty-five thousand livres it was possible to buy an estate or stocks producing enough revenue to support several preachers. Not without some resistance, Monsieur Vincent accepted the role they wished to entrust to him.

Obviously it was not a question of founding a religious order. The project was much more modest. The number of preachers was limited to six, in keeping with the revenue from the capital invested. Chance—or was it once again an act of Providence?—so arranged it that Jean François de Gondi, the brother of the General of the Galleys, was head of the Paris archdiocese; it even happened that his title was archiepiscopal. For his sister-in-law's work he offered a college, rather small, it must be admitted, near the Porte Saint-Victor, the Collège des Bons Enfants. Monsieur Vincent was appointed as principal and took pos-

session on March 2, 1624, but left the actual work of direction to his first companion, Father Portail. The Gondis were much too afraid of losing their chaplain!

Nevertheless, everything was prepared for the foundation in view. A careful contract was drawn up and signed, on April 17, 1625, with the names of General and Madame de Gondi. It dealt not only with money and administrative measures; spiritual matters played a foremost role in the preamble. Allusion was made to the spiritual destitution of the countryside, whereas people in the cities had the benefits of preaching and instruction in catechism from a number of priests and doctors of the Church. Not that clergy were lacking in the outlying districts, but they were often unequal to their task through ignorance and negligence.

Monsieur and Madame de Gondi thought to remedy this "by a pious association of priests, well-founded in doctrine, piety and of known ability, who would renounce their city life as well as all the benefits, charges and dignities of the Church, each with the permission of the prelates and within the boundaries of his diocese, in order to apply themselves entirely and purely to the salvation of poor people, going from village to village at the expense of their common purse, to preach, instruct, exhort and teach catechism to these poor folk . . ." The contract also went into details; Monsieur Vincent must have taken a hand in drawing it up. ". . . the said ecclesiastics," said the text, "shall live in community under obedience to the said Sieur du Paul, and to their future superiors after his death, with the name of the company, congregation or confraternity of the *Fathers of the Priests of the Mission.*"

To be fair, we must concede that at this time such an undertaking was not unheard of. At the end of the previous century, an admirable Jesuit, Father Auger, had preached missions throughout the south of France from Pamiers to Tournon, and in Bordeaux. His catechism had such success he was called the "French Canisius," in memory of the work of another Jesuit in Germany. Still another Jesuit, Father Francis Regis, worked so heroically among the mountaineers of Velay that he was to die young, of exhaustion, at La Louvesc. Father Véron was going about the country near Caen; the amazing Michel Le Nobletz was active in Britanny, opening the way for Father Maunoir. Monsieur Vincent was not alone in this work, but he was then alone—although St. John Eudes would soon follow him—in giving an institutional form to his undertaking.

Two months after signing the contract, the good Madame de Gondi died, and a year later her husband joined the Oratorians. Monsieur Vincent therefore found himself free to devote himself to the new work and to rejoin his first companions at the Collège des Bons Enfants. At first the company counted only four members: Vincent de Paul,

Antoine Portail, François Ducoudray and Jean de la Salle. A little afterward four others came: Jean Bécu, Antoine Lucas, Jean Brunet and Jean d'Horgny. All were well educated men, several of them doctors of the Sorbonne.

To the sincere surprise of the founder, the "confraternity" grew larger. In 1626 it was possible to establish itself as a "congregation," to obtain letters of patent from the king authorizing it to accept alms and donations for its work. Finally, thanks to the ability of Father Ducoudray, sent expressly to Rome for the purpose, the Holy See, disregarding the little acrimonies caused by the new foundation, was ready to give its approval. This was done on January 12, 1632, by the bull *Salvatori nostro* signed by Urban VIII.

No one was more astonished than Monsieur Vincent at this success, these rapid steps forward. Twenty years later he was to write: "We were going just plainly and simply to preach the Gospel to the poor as Our Lord had done. That is what we were doing, and God did, on His side, what He had foreseen from all eternity. He gave some blessings on our work which other good ecclesiastics saw, and they wished to join us. . . . Oh, Saviour! who would ever have thought that this would come to its present state? If anyone had told me so at that time I would have thought he was making fun of me. And nevertheless this was the way God wanted our company to begin. Well, can you call human something no man had ever thought of? For neither I nor poor Monsieur Portail ever thought of it; very far from it!"

In the same year of 1632, the year the bull was granted, in the same month of January, another providential event occurred. There was in Paris an old leprosarium which no longer had any patients, but which still housed eight canons of St. Victor under the direction of their prior, Adrien le Bon. It was called Saint-Lazare, after the patron saint of lepers. Old and tired and moreover on bad terms with his religious, the prior wished to get rid of the place. He offered Monsieur Vincent the vast building, actually in very bad condition, and the immense lands attached to it. At first Vincent de Paul refused it: "We are poor priests, we live simply, our only ambition is to serve the poor country people. . . ." He also added: "We have only just started, we are but a handful."

But again it was impossible not to respond to an obvious solicitation from Providence. Monsieur Vincent's closest adviser, Monsieur du Val, persuaded him to accept. The contract was therefore signed and the Priests of the Mission went to take up residence at Saint-Lazare. This is the origin of the name *Lazaristes* by which they are called in France and in Italy (whereas in Spain they are known as *Padres Paules* and in America as *Vincentians*).

Originally they were secular priests who banded together to take on a definite task—missions in the country districts. They were to go into the rural

53

parishes to preach in each place for one month, between October and June; during the summer, when the fieldworkers were very busy, they would devote themselves to teaching catechism to the children, preaching at Sunday Masses, helping the pastors who wished it. One point on which Monsieur Vincent insisted was that each one "work for his own perfection, practicing the virtues that the Sovereign Master taught us by word and example," so that they would be able to take on their missionary work. The true role Monsieur Vincent assigned his companions was of acting as the leaven in the bread.

Thus he wrote, on December 17, 1638, to Father de Sergis, a priest of the Mission, then in Toulouse: "Everyone says that the missionary spirit is a spirit of humility and simplicity: hold to this; the spirit of meekness, of simplicity and humility is the spirit of Our Lord." He wished his sons to be close to the poor people they met, able to live the same lives, above all, to be understood by them.

The simplicity he required was first that of language. Monsieur Vincent held in horror flowery oratory, affectation, pomposity, and quotations from the Latin. The necessary thing was to speak from the heart and to the heart. "To flaunt around fine phrases," he exclaimed, "is to commit a sacrilege!" To one of his Sons who did not seem to have regarded his advice, he wrote not without irony: "I have been told that you put yourself to too much effort in speaking to the people, and that this has greatly weakened you. In the name of God, Monsieur, think of your health and moderate your words and your feelings! I have told you that Our Lord blesses the sermon which is preached in an ordinary and familiar tone, because He Himself taught and preached in that way; and the people prefer and draw more profit from that manner of speaking because it is natural and also easier than the other, which is forced." Monsieur Vincent, the reformer of preaching!

It goes without saying Monsieur Vincent wished his companions to receive nothing for the missions they preached. Let other preachers be paid for their sermons! In 1647, when the Congregation was fully established and their ministrations in wide demand, he learned that a very noble lady wished to compensate the Missionaries of Coulommiers. Immediately he wrote to Father Delville, the superior: "You tell me that Madame de Longueville wishes to pay expenses. Oh, my God, Monsieur, must we begin to dissipate and ruin the spirit of the Mission! Oh, Jesus, may God not allow you to be the instrument of such a misfortune! We are no less obliged to give our missions for nothing than the Capuchins are to live on alms. Oh, my God, what could one say of a Capuchin who was concerned with money that could not be said of a missionary who permitted himself to be paid!"

It was because of such wisdom and generosity that the work succeeded. The missionaries threw all their efforts into their work everywhere they

preached. First of all, it goes without saying, was Monsieur Vincent himself. At his process of canonization, Bossuet was to testify to the indelible impression made on his soul at a mission given by the future saint. But the same was true of the others, those who followed his example. To all he said, over and over, that their first, their only duty was to make themselves loved by those around them. "We do not believe a man because he is learned, but because we esteem and love him"—his letters abound with such phrases. It seems his disciples understood and obeyed him, for their success was immense. Within a few years Vincent's Mission had become an institution in all of France.

A mission was an event in every village and canton where they preached. It even happened, as in Laon, that fairs and markets were closed down so that everyone could attend. Day after day for at least three weeks, the band of missionaries would work the region, speaking not only in the church, but also outside the church, in the squares, at street corners, and visiting homes. Sometimes the beginning was difficult. One missionary wrote from Poitiers: "These souls, which seemed hard as stone, have taken on the sacred fire." Because it did not take long for them to arouse enthusiasm, the good people hastened to the confessional, then to the holy table.

Thus, in turn, or simultaneously, dioceses such as Mende, Arles, Angoulême, Cahors, Sens, Annecy, Châlons, Trégier, Guingamp, Morlaix, became their fields of action, nor did they forget the region around Paris. Everywhere the good seed was sown. From his little room at Saint-Lazare, Monsieur Vincent followed this immense activity, holding in his own hands the lines of operation, writing minute instructions to the missionaries carrying on this work, then going to read to his beloved novices the letters, often very beautiful, received from the fighters in the field. Sometimes they were moved to tears: for example, when he read aloud a letter from Father Etienne Blatiron, missioner in Corsica, telling how, after one of his sermons, two enemies divided by a cruel vendetta threw themselves into one another's arms in the presence of the greatly moved congregation.

It even came about that Monsieur Vincent consented to depart from his principle of concerning themselves only with country people, when he considered that the Mission would be useful elsewhere. So, in 1638, he agreed to spread his work to other places and to send preachers to the far from model Christians peopling the royal parish of Saint-Germain. These preachers were chosen from among the best of his auditors at his *Conferences du Mardi* (Tuesday Conferences)—we will hear more of this activity of Vincent's later—and they were directed to spare neither the noble lords who engaged in duels, nor the fine ladies who went about with "breasts uncovered." Three years later he accepted such an invitation from the curé of Saint-Sulpice, then a suburban Parisian parish, and

reputed to be "the sink of all the iniquities." This
curé was none other than Father Olier.

Figures do not give a sufficient idea of this immense effort. However, these figures are eloquent. At Monsieur Vincent's death in 1660, 840 missions had been given by Saint-Lazare. The Congregation had 23 houses, with 131 priests and clerics and 52 brother helpers. So great was the impetus given by the founder that at the end of the century there were 53 houses, and at the time of the French Revolution, 66. And—a final triumph —there was, even during the lifetime of the saint, a house in Rome, a house on which the Pope himself bestowed signal favors. "Three makes more than ten, when Our Lord takes a hand in things," remarked Monsieur Vincent with his best smile. It was very true that He had taken a hand in the Mission.

To preach to the people was not enough, and Monsieur Vincent knew this better than anyone. He had come to realize in Folleville as in Châtillon that the most profound cause of the low religious level of the people was the degradation of the clergy. Words which came frequently from his lips and pen were: "Christianity depends on the priests." A holy clergy, Blanc de Saint-Bonnet was to say later, makes a virtuous people. . . .

It must be admitted that the French clergy at that time, as elsewhere all over Christendom, had great need to relearn the ways to sanctity! The

Council of Trent had seen the problem and measured its gravity; it had opened up the way for the future by deciding to found seminaries for the training of priests. Still, its decisions had to be put into operation before the spirit that animated the Fathers of the Council could pass into the marrow of the Church.

Monsieur Vincent had no illusions as to the enormity of the task to be accomplished in this regard. No one knew better than he the deplorable state of the French clergy, especially of the rural clergy. There was a saying current in Provence: "If you want to go to hell, make yourself a priest!" Was this only popular malice?

We hear such remarks as these from the mouth of Monsieur Vincent himself: "Priests living in the way most of them do today are the greatest enemies of the Church of God." Or again: "The depravity of the ecclesiastical state is the principal cause of the ruin of the Church." Perhaps he was exaggerating a bit; he was among those who vomit out the lukewarm, and a priest who did not give himself body and soul to his vocation appeared unworthy to Monsieur Vincent. "Ah," he said again, "if a good priest can do so much good, oh, how much evil is done by a bad priest!" And, as though in a prayer, he ended with this little sentence in which one hears, as it were in advance, the saintly Curé d'Ars: "There is nothing so grand as a good priest."

Therefore one of the major tasks he proposed to his sons was to raise and train good priests. "Oh, sirs my brothers, the training of good ecclesiastics is the most difficult, the highest and the most important work for the salvation of souls." Again it was necessary—according to the principle so dear to Monsieur Vincent—for the Lord visibly to manifest His desire to entrust him with such cares, him and his Sons. One day in July 1628, the bishop of Beauvais, Monseigneur Augustin Potier de Gesvres, was rolling along in his commodious coach in the company of several ecclesiastics, among them our Vincent. The prelate had closed his eyes and seemed to be asleep. Suddenly, he opened them and exclaimed: "At last I see a quick and effectual way to prepare clerics for holy orders. I will have them come to my residence for several days. They will devote themselves to pious exercises and will be instructed in their duties and functions."

"This idea comes from God, Monseigneur," Vincent de Paul replied with enthusiasm, "and I can see nothing better myself as a means for setting your clergy on the right road."

"It would be well to start as soon as possible," the bishop went on. "Draw up a program, prepare a list of subjects for the talks, and fifteen or twenty days before the ordinations in September, come to Beauvais to get everything ready for the retreat."

This was done, and thus began the training sessions, the *Retreats for Ordinands* as they were then called, which were the cradles of the seminaries. For Monsieur Vincent the principal object of these retreats was to test the reality of vocations. It was important not to admit anyone into holy orders without the moral assurance that he had been called to the priesthood by God. In the second place, future priests must be seriously instructed

regarding the responsibilities awaiting them and inculcated with a sense of the meaning of the words, "the charge of souls."

Vincent thereupon prepared a program in his well-known manner: a profound view of the whole, attention to the least detail. The program was judged so perfect that from Beauvais it passed little by little to the other dioceses. In February, 1631, the Archbishop of Paris asked the originator of the method personally to undertake the direction of aspirants to holy orders in his archdiocese; the Collège des Bons Enfants, at that time still the motherhouse of the Priests of the Mission, appeared to him to be the best place for the experiment.

Once again Monsieur Vincent tried to shun a responsibility that seemed to him very heavy. He had the care of the galley slaves, whose chaplain general he was; of the rapidly increasing groups of the Ladies of Charity; of his own growing confraternity; not to mention the Visitation nuns entrusted to him by the Bishop of Geneva. . . . The archbishop insisted, and Monsieur Vincent had to surrender in face of the Lord's evident wish that he should take a part in the formation of the clergy of Paris.

So was begun in 1631, during Lent, at the Bons Enfants, and continued during the following years at Saint-Lazare, the Retreat for Ordinands to which so many excellent priests of the century of Louis XIV owed their formation. The "session" lasted only twenty days; things had to proceed at a fast pace. The ordinands were received by the Priests of the Mission, fed and lodged gratis. For three weeks they had only to think of their spiritual advancement. Each day they heard two lectures, one in the morning on moral theology, another in the evening on the functions of holy orders and the virtues required of them. After each talk, the ordinands met together in groups of twelve or fifteen, in "conferences" where they discussed with the teacher the subject on which he spoke. The Priest of the Mission then asked questions. . . .

The results of these retreats were extraordinary. On July 5, 1633, Vincent de Paul described them in the following way to his friend Ducoudray who was at that time in Rome: "You should know," he said, "that it has pleased the good God to give a particular blessing, one that can hardly be imagined, to the exercises of our ordinands. It is such that all, or almost all, who have followed them are living a life which should be that of good and perfect ecclesiastics. There are even some of high birth or other qualities given them by God who live in their own homes lives as well regulated as our own. They regulate their time, devote themselves to mental prayer, celebrate Holy Mass, examine their consciences daily as we do. They visit hospitals and prisons, where they catechize, preach, hear confessions as they do also in the colleges, all with the special blessings of God. Among them are twelve or fifteen who live in this way and who are persons of rank—this is beginning to be publicly known."

In the meantime this institution continued to make its way all over the country and even beyond the borders of France. Vincent's method was soon used in a good third of the French dioceses, in Savoy, and even in Rome. The Retreats for Ordinands were to last until 1643, the date when the general foundation of seminaries rendered them much less necessary. But one of their results was to last a long time afterward.

This was the *Conférences du Mardi*. The request for these reunions came to Monsieur Vincent from certain of the priests who had followed the retreats preparatory to ordination. Immediately they realized that three weeks of formation and instruction were a very slim foundation for the whole existence of a priest. They therefore asked their master to bring them together at Saint-Lazare "to confer with them regarding the virtues and functions proper to their ministry." On June 11, 1633, Monsieur Vincent explained to his chosen auditors his plan for the Conferences. On June 24, he began the cycle. On July 9, it was decided they should be held every Tuesday: at Saint-Lazare from Easter to All Saints' Day, the rest of the time at the Collège des Bons Enfants. The rule specified that only ecclasiastics belonging to the secular clergy could be admitted—religious were excluded since their training was the duty of their order. All those who inscribed must come regularly, only legitimate excuses would be accepted. The subjects treated would be of three kinds: Christian virtues, the

duties of ecclesiastics, the charges and dignities of the Church. Each would speak in turn on the subject proposed, but for only a quarter of an hour. The session would not last longer than two hours. This was the regular procedure which began on July 16, 1633.

A slight idea of the influence of this unique undertaking may be reached when we point out that among the auditors most constant in attendance were such men as Bossuet (from 1643 onward); Pavillon, the future bishop of Alet; Father Olier, founder of the Sulpicians; nor must we forget the "tempestuous Abbé" Rancé, future reformer of the Cistercian order at Grande Trappe. There is little doubt that the renewal of the art of pulpit oratory must be dated from the Tuesday Conferences; to them must also be attributed the start of the slow work of rehabilitating all of France's clergy—because the Tuesday Conferences were imitated in a great number of other dioceses. Even when they did not meet with the striking success of those in Paris, since there was only one Monsieur Vincent, they exerted everywhere a salutary influence.

This influence also went beyond the small circles of the ranking clergy who felt the need of this advanced training. At Saint-Lazare and later in other Lazarist houses, Monsieur Vincent instituted "closed retreats" of the sort conceived by St. Ignatius of Loyola, and to these were admitted not only all priests and religious who desired it, but men living in the world, rich or poor without distinc-

tion. As always he set up for these retreats a rule from which nothing was omitted. For these retreatants—or *exercitants* as he called them—he provided everything that could make the period of the retreat profitable and even agreeable, right up to the nightcap which each must have at his disposal.

"Oh, gentlemen," he said to his Lazarists, "how highly we should esteem the grace God gives us when He leads so many people to us so that we can help them to their salvation. Even soldiers are coming, and recently one of them said to me, 'Monsieur, I soon have to face an emergency and I wish to be in a proper state.'" How many worthy men came during those years to the Lazarist retreats asking for the opportunity to face more bravely "the emergencies" of death and of life!

However, as we see it in perspective, the Retreats for Ordinands, even when carried further by the Tuesday Conferences, were not enough. A priest is not trained in three weeks and his fervor is not maintained by a weekly conference. The Council of Trent had commanded the foundation of seminaries but, to tell the truth, the Fathers remained rather vague as to the application of this excellent principle. It was not sufficient to open houses, nor even to place in them carefully recruited professors and arrange for studies not provided for in the universities properly so called. A formula must be found to make these really living institutions, to draw up rules for material and spiritual purposes, to build up a world of customs for which no earlier tradition existed.

Certainly Monsieur Vincent was not the only one in France to think of this. Cardinal de Bérulle felt it as a pressing duty; Vincent's contemporaries, such as Father Olier and St. John Eudes, had the same desire as he to bring it to fruition. And in his priory-rectory at Saint-Nicolas du Chardonnet, Father Adrien Bourdoise had already accomplished a great deal. But none of the efforts made before had produced very good results. For twenty-two years Bérulle's Oratorians had made attempt after attempt with such mediocre success that they were going to start another more promising work: the education of youth. At Saint-Nicolas du Chardonnet the future priests being trained by the community were necessarily limited in number. Something else must be done. The priests—some of whom had become bishops—trained by Monsieur Vincent, begged him to take on this urgent task.

This was an enormous undertaking. Did God expect it of him? Mindful of the good accomplished by his missions in the country, Vincent asked himself this. Again Providence supplied— and imposed on him—the reply. This came through Cardinal de Richelieu's personal intervention. During a memorable audience the great minister asked the founder of the Lazarists to harness himself to this work. How could he refuse?

And so it was that the Collège des Bons Enfants —by a curious coincidence situated not a hundred yards away from Father Bourdoise's rectory—became a seminary. The fundamental idea, once again showing the realistic genius of the saint, was to distinguish between what we call "major seminarians" and "minor seminarians." The Council of Trent had not made this distinction, and an ambiguous passage in one of its canons, drawn up during the twenty-third session, had let it be assumed that boys of all ages from twelve onward should be admitted into the future seminaries. This St. Charles Borromeo in Milan, Cardinal de Lorraine in Rheims, and Bérulle's Oratorians had tried to do. The results were not outstanding; the mixture of boys and young men of twenty-two or twenty-three was not a happy one.

Monsieur Vincent kept the "major seminarians," a dozen young men in their first year's training, at the Bons Enfants, and started at Saint-Lazare a school for the younger lads, a real "minor seminary." This was called the School of St. Charles and it was installed in one of the annexes of the motherhouse of the Priests of the Mission. He even decided that the children who came to follow the courses were not obliged to enter the priesthood: a liberal intention much in advance of his time, and having as its object the training of Christian lay leaders. A definite pattern for the seminaries had been found, and this at the same time that Father Olier, after other experiments, reached the same conclusions. This pattern thereafter was definitive in France.

We must admit that these early major seminaries were not like our present ones. The length of residence, now six years, was much less and it also varied according to the diocese and the institution: between six months and two years. The training amounted in fact to an extension of the Retreats for Ordinands rather than to a complete and systematic preparation. Intellectual education was little stressed; emphasis was placed on pastoral and spiritual formation. Also the rule provided by Monsieur Vincent in person would appear rather Draconian today—especially with regard to the hours for rising, the number of spiritual exercises, the fasting and penances. It is nonetheless true that from these first Vincentian seminaries—as also from the seminaries of the Sulpicians and Eudists —there issued an élite of priests such as France had not known for three centuries and who were long unrivaled by the priests of any other country.

The Lazarist seminaries multiplied: Cahors in 1643, Saintes in 1644, Mans in 1645, Agen and Tréguier in 1648, Montauban in 1649. . . . When Monsieur Vincent died there were coming from "his" seminaries each year more than four hundred priests trained according to his methods.

In Monsieur Vincent's mind the reconquest of souls in the name of Christ was inseparable from another task: aid to the body. In those days at

Châtillon he had thrown his efforts into charitable enterprises in order to revive his parish spiritually. For him the two efforts were inseparable. In all of what we would call in our day the "social work" of Monsieur Vincent we must always see in the end and as the only effective motive a love that surpasses all earthly loves and relates everything to Christ.

The organization of the *Ladies of Charity* that sprang up through providential chance in Châtillon, in 1617, the organization for which he set up from the start the most solid rules, had not ceased to make progress. Almost everywhere similar groups were being formed of young married women, widows, young girls, who without leading in any way the existence of nuns, sought to bring help to "our lords the poor." Monsieur Vincent's appeals had met with much good will. And among these women could be found France's greatest names: the Princess Montmorency, the Duchess of Nemours, the wealthy Madame Goussault, Madame de Maupeou and Madame de Miramion. The Queen herself came often to care with her own hands for the sick in the poorest hospitals. Louise de Marillac belonged to this troop of well-doers, although God held in store for her a vocation higher still.

What was done by these Ladies of Charity? In a word, they did everything that could ease human miseries, including the most repellent, the most hideous. For each of the groups, Monsieur Vincent

established a rule in accordance with his usual cus-
tom. Here is a sample of the detail the saint went
into:

"Each sick person should have as much bread as
he needs, with a quarter pound of boiled mutton or
beef for dinner, and the same amount of roast for
supper; except on Sundays when they may be given
some boiled chicken for their dinner, and two or
three times a week their meat may be chopped.
Those who have no fever should have a pint of wine
each day, half in the morning and half in the evening. On Fridays, Saturdays and other days of ab-
stinence they should have two eggs and soup and a
little slice of butter for dinner, and the same quan-
tity for their supper, adjusting the number of eggs
to their appetites. If fish can be found at an honest
price, this shall be given them only at dinner. Permission to eat meat in Lent and on other forbidden
days should be obtained for those who are very ill;
and if they are unable to eat solid meat, they should
be given bouillon, bread-soup or toasted bread, bar-
ley gruel and fresh eggs, twice or thrice a day."

The mother of a family could have taken no
more trouble to regulate the food of her children.
In reading such lines as these we think of the
"higher realism" considered by Bergson as one of
the outstanding virtues of the great mystics. Strictly
organized as they were, the Ladies of Charity were
astonishingly successful. Ten years after Châtillon
there were a hundred such groups across France.
However, with the men, Monsieur Vincent was

less fortunate; in those days when violence was widespread, the males considered charitable tasks as the work of women. It was for Frederic Ozanam to succeed two hundred years later where the originator had failed, but it was to be exactly in the same spirit and following in his footsteps that the young and saintly professor was to found the "Conferences of St. Vincent de Paul" which were then to meet with so much success.

The Ladies of Charity were however only the *avant garde*. From their work, through a natural filiation often met in the way of Monsieur Vincent, another work was born, its development and influence to be even more vast: the institute of the *Daughters of Charity*. At this point another name must be associated with Monsieur Vincent's, that of Louise de Marillac. Together these two saintly figures labored to bring this work into being; together they watched over its development. Even today there are still disputes as to which one took the initiative. It was doutbless from humility that the foundress wished to remain in the shadow of the founder, and this shadow is so deep that to posterity the daughters of Louise de Marillac are still known as the "Sisters of St. Vincent de Paul."

Who was this modest young woman? A young widow who, at the age of thirty-four, had just lost her husband, Antoine Le Gras. Instead of shutting herself up in her sorrow and the care of her only son—or, on the other hand, giving herself over to distractions—this courageous daughter of Auvergne wished to spend her life in doing something useful. This resolution may even have antedated her bereavement if it is true, as she was to say later, that one day very soon after her marriage it had been revealed to her that the day would come when she could "take the vow of poverty, chastity and obedience." "But," she added, "I could not understand how this could be, for I could see many comings and goings." This meant that the congregation to which she would belong would not be cloistered—at that time an inconceivable idea.

Evidently prepared and directed by Providence, Mademoiselle Le Gras—for thus she was called, since at that time the title "Madame" was reserved for wives and daughters of the ranking nobility—recognized, once she was widowed, God's call in a very particular direction, namely the one to be pointed out to her by Monsieur Vincent. An interior voice impelled her to entrust herself to him, and yet she hesitated: "I felt repugnance in accepting this," she confessed. Nevertheless she submitted, and from 1624 onward, the saint directed her. He knew perfectly how to quiet her impatience, to teach her how to trust in Providence, and to do everything "plainly and simply."

Five years went by, and it is probable that since she was active in the work of the Ladies of Charity, Monsieur Vincent had time to examine and form an opinion of his penitent. In 1629, having measured her decided abilities, he entrusted her with an important post. It was no less than the task of going to inspect all the groups of Ladies of Charity set up in the provinces, to see whether they were working more or less well, to supervise, correct or reform them. In this way Mademoiselle became the soul of the movement, the founder's right hand in this vast undertaking.

As realistic as he was himself, Mademoiselle soon recognized that the organization of the confraternity of the Ladies suffered from various defects. First it was difficult to compel women of the world to strict attention to charitable tasks; moreover, it was even harder to submit them all to those menial and often humiliating labors required in caring for the poor. Louise de Marillac therefore suggested to Monsieur Vincent the desirability of joining to the Ladies of Charity helpers recruited preferably from among country people accustomed to hard work. This idea seemed so excellent to the founder that he had sent, or himself brought from his missions several of "these good village girls" as he called them, whose simplicity, humility, submissiveness and disinterestedness appeared exemplary to him. This was the beginning of the *Daughters of Charity*.

A definite pattern for the institute was not found immediately. At first an attempt was made simply to divide the helpers among the various companies of the Ladies; the results were mediocre. The helpers had to be trained and grouped in such a way they would not feel lost in strange surroundings. Louise de Marillac, at that time presiding officer of the Charity of Saint-Nicolas in Paris, took several of the girls into her home. That was in November 1633—a date that may be regarded as that of the beginning of the new institute. Without delay, Monsieur Vincent provided them with a rule. The motto he proposed for them was striking in its brevity: "Leave God for God." This was to say, "Leave prayer to go to the poor, who are the representatives of God, since Christ identified Himself with them." The dual love, affective and effective, was to be found in them.

During twenty-seven years, from 1633 to 1660, with tireless care, Vincent took part in the direction of the Daughters of Charity, regularly giving them the "conferences" which later filled two enormous volumes and where perhaps the most beautiful pages of his writings are to be found. Very often he came back to the idea of the two loves. "You should love Our Lord tenderly and affectionately, as does a child who cannot be separated from his mother and cries 'Mama' the moment she wishes to go away." This was for the affective love. But also: "The love of the Daughters of Charity is not only tender; it is effective, because they serve effectively the poor, corporally and spiritually . . . To give oneself to God in order to serve Him in the person of the poor"—such were the aims, strictly insep-arable, of the new religious group.

Religious: the word that comes naturally to our lips today in speaking of the Daughters of Mon-sieur Vincent would not have seemed appropriate

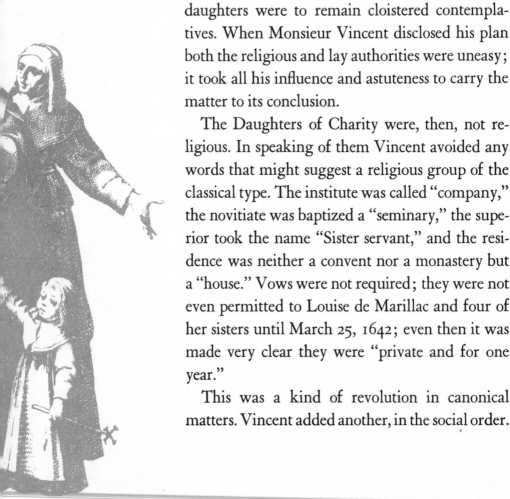

to him. In the canonical meaning of the term they were not religious. To tell the truth, this foundation was revolutionary. In his day no one conceived of a feminine vocation outside the cloister: Claretians, Carmelites, Dominicans were nuns living out of the world, enclosed in their convents. The idea of an institute for women living in the world had occurred, as we saw, to St. Francis de Sales when he founded the Visitation with Jeanne de Chantal. The lack of understanding of the archbishop of Lyons had prevented the bishop of Annecy and Geneva from realizing his project, and his daughters were to remain cloistered contemplatives. When Monsieur Vincent disclosed his plan both the religious and lay authorities were uneasy; it took all his influence and astuteness to carry the matter to its conclusion.

The Daughters of Charity were, then, not religious. In speaking of them Vincent avoided any words that might suggest a religious group of the classical type. The institute was called "company," the novitiate was baptized a "seminary," the superior took the name "Sister servant," and the residence was neither a convent nor a monastery but a "house." Vows were not required; they were not even permitted to Louise de Marillac and four of her sisters until March 25, 1642; even then it was made very clear they were "private and for one year."

This was a kind of revolution in canonical matters. Vincent added another, in the social order.

Until that time charitable activities were reserved either to clerics—for example, the Brothers of St. John of God—or to women of society. The sublime road was now opened to the daughters of the common people. For it was above all the children of the people who filled the ranks of the new institute. We have only to read the lists to be convinced of this: Madeleine Raporteblé, Marie Vigneron, Jeanne Grésier, Mathurine Guérin, Toussaint David, Françoise Fanchon—all names with the aroma of France's soil.

Their apparel was exactly what the peasants wore in that day: a full grayish dress, cloak of the same color and the white cornette so often seen in the Ile-de-France. Hence the name "Gray Sisters,"[1] given them by the people, and which seems inaccurate to us today because since the French Revolution the cloak has been blue.

They had scarcely been founded when the Daughters of Charity revealed their prodigious adaptability. There was truly no form of misery they did not concern themselves with nor try to relieve. Soon they were to be found in hospitals and hospices and in the frightful pens where the galley-slaves waited to embark on the royal ships; they were also to be found with the armies where several of them served as the first women nurses.

[1] We remember Napoleon's words. When someone spoke in his presence of the benefits of philanthropy in the Age of Enlightenment the Emperor interrupted, saying, "All that is good and well, gentlemen, but give us a Gray Sister any time."

The work of teaching children so stressed in the Church at that time—education appearing as the most eminent means of training the young in their faith—was likewise familiar to them; they became teachers just as readily as they became nurses.

Is it possible to find examples among so much hidden sanctity and discreet heroism? Perhaps we should speak of "Sister Marie Joseph" who in 1652, after having spent two years on the battlefields of Picardy and Champagne, arrived at Etampes where the misery was immense, and spent all her strength in combating it. She could hardly stand on her feet, she was exhausted and ill but until the end she visited the sick and the poor; when she could no longer stand on her feet she had them brought to her so that she could still give them her care, then she lay down and died. Or again, we might speak of the amazing Marguerite Naseau, the little cowherd of Surennes, who learned the alphabet alone—its letters were then called "the crosses of God"—and taught herself the little she was able, then went from village to village to pass on to the country children what she had learned. Monsieur Vincent found her thus engaged at Ville-preux, and, marveling at her devotion and untiring charity, was to call her "the first daughter of charity."

Thus separated from the Ladies of Charity, the new institute prospered. The customary rule was put into writing. In 1646 and 1655 it was approved by the Archbishop of Paris; he was another Gondi, the youngest of the sons of Monsieur Vincent's friends. Under the name of Cardinal de Retz, he was to acquire a rather doubtful reputation, but he played a beneficent role in connection with Monsieur Vincent's institute. Royal letters of patent in 1657, registered by Parliament the following year, gave the institute its legal standing in France while it awaited full approval in Rome. This approbation was given in 1718, at which time the definitive constitutions were promulgated. By then the Gray Sisters had become numerous and powerful. When Monsieur Vincent died in 1660, they had fifty-one houses; in 1700, three hundred, with a thousand Sisters. At the time of the French Revolution there were more than four thousand five hundred Sisters. Today there are forty-five thousand—the largest institute of women in the Church.

Such were the helpers Monsieur Vincent found at his side in his works of charity—works so numerous that they can scarcely be counted. Even in mentioning the principal ones we can merely give an idea of the variety of fields tended by their ever watchful care.

The hospitals. Their conditions in those days were far from good. Their organization was mediocre, they were terribly overcrowded; personnel and care of the sick were insufficient. When, in 1634, Madame Goussault took him to see with his own eyes the deplorable state of the Hôtel-Dieu, Monsieur Vincent reached an immediate decision. He called a hundred of his Ladies of Charity to take the hospital under their charge; although the **Gray** Sisters had just been founded and were not yet numerous, they immediately came to help. The Hôtel-Dieu was to become the model hospital of Paris.

Foundlings. In the Paris of that day they were countless; thousands of abandoned children were gathered up each year. The so-called receiving center for them known as *La Couche* gave them over to anybody, sometimes to professional beggars who mutilated them so they would help them to arouse pity. In 1638, Louise de Marillac started a new charity and Monsieur Vincent went begging for funds with such persuasiveness that his Ladies of Charity broke down and wept. After its foundation in 1660, the Hospital for Foundlings received no less than forty thousand little ones.

Another plague of Paris was its swarming beggars. Many were sick, mutilated, crippled. They had to be taken off the streets and, when that was done, not treated as common lawbreakers—as certain people were inclined to do. A first hospital was opened for them with forty beds; then the "Little Houses," a place to receive syphilitics, was put under the charge of the Gray Sisters. Next was the Salpêtrière, a hospital given by Queen Anne of Austria to Monsieur Vincent and his daughters.

There was no form of distress that did not appeal to the charitable heart of the saint. There were no lower dregs of humanity than the convicts. The prison life of that period was abominable. And what was worst, into these dungeons were thrown pell-mell with bandits those who had been con- demned for non-payment of debts, or the sons of good families who had committed indiscretions. Monsieur Vincent went in person to visit these unfortunates; then he went to see those in power and demanded justice for them. At least, he asked, could they not have spiritual aid, and why could not a prison chaplaincy be created? And for delinquent adolescents he opened at Saint-Lazare a house of rehabilitation.

Perhaps even more dramatic was the fate of the galley-slaves who rowed the royal ships. Monsieur Vincent had seen them at close range when he was chaplain general of the galleys. He had protested loudly against the brutality of the "committees" who, with whip in hand, pressed them to faster speed. He sent Daughters of Charity to help these poor galley-slaves whom he could not forget. One of the Daughters, Barbe Angiboust, was to become famous among them for her gentleness, generosity and patience.

Where would Monsieur Vincent's charity stop? Not even before the Turks. In Barbary, he knew from experience, there were Christian slaves, completely abandoned. One must go to see and console them. And if the Mussulman authorities opposed this, the obstacle could be met by asking the King of France to appoint missionaries as consuls so they could go to Africa. This was done with the Lazarist Jean Le Vacher, vicar general of Carthage

and consul of France who, after accomplishing much good, ended his life as a martyr, tied before the mouth of a Turkish canon.

Thus, with the heroic figure of Jean Le Vacher, appeared the fourth great aspect of Monsieur Vincent's multiform work: participation in the evangelization of distant lands. A great chapter was opening in the history of the Church, a new impetus was being given to the spreading of the Christian message. The foundation, in 1622, of the Congregation of the Propaganda had proved that the Papacy intended taking into its own hands the work of evangelization. Following in the footsteps of St. Francis Xavier, missionaries were in Asia; Africa was being opened to Christ; penetration into Latin America was constant; and Father Olier was preparing to send his Sulpicians to Canada.

Monsieur Vincent could not remain outside this current, neither he nor his Sons and Daughters. However, he did not show any haste—the peasants of France, the poor and the abandoned were his immediate concern. Here again, as on every occasion, he would not decide until Providence let him know clearly that action was expected of him. He was nonetheless passionately interested in the missionary effort into which the clergy of France was beginning to throw its efforts. Father Joseph, Richelieu's "Gray Eminence," found a friend and supporter in Vincent when he conceived of his great missions in the Near East and entrusted them to the Capuchins. And when the Congregation of the Propaganda called upon the French to go to the Far East to carry out the papal directives and the first vicars apostolic were appointed, Monsieur Vincent supported with all his authority the efforts of the young priests who volunteered for this task. Monseigneur François Pallu, a founder of the Society of Foreign Missions, no doubt owed much to him, as did his Society before which lay so brilliant a future.

On two occasions, however, the voice of Providence became imperious. In 1646, it was heard through Pope Innocent X, who invited Monsieur Vincent to send his Sons not to a pagan country but to a very old Christian land at that time threatened by heresy and where Catholics were in need of help. This was Ireland—"Hibernia" as it was then called. The danger came from Protestantism as embodied in the Puritan Cromwell. It was the Pope's idea for the Lazarist missionaries to strengthen the ties between Catholics in order for them better to face the peril, and at the same time by their charity and effective zeal to bring back to the Catholic Church its sons who had strayed.

Perhaps this plan was visionary. The old country of St. Patrick and St. Columban received with enthusiasm these priests of a new type who seemed to bring them the aid of a younger Christianity. But the Lazarists did not have time to pursue their activities. The revolution in England, imposing

Cromwell's dictatorship, brought down upon the Emerald Isle the savage attacks of the "Roundheads." St. Vincent's Sons were dispersed and forced to flee, but not without leaving a deep imprint on the Irish soil where the Lazarists have since become numerous.

Almost at the same time—another sign from heaven—Bagni, the papal nuncio in Paris, handed Monsieur Vincent a request from the Company of the Indies for priests to be sent to Madagascar, an island where the Company held a monopoly over commerce. The founder of the Lazarists did not think he should turn a deaf ear to this appeal.

There then opened in the history of the young Company of the Mission a glorious page and one singularly characteristic of the intentions and methods of its founder. The island was administered by a governor named Flacourt, the embodiment of the worst spirit of colonialism; to him the natives were less than human. The two Fathers sent by Monsieur Vincent to the island quite evidently did not share such prejudices; they were the brilliant young Father Nacquart and the humble, sincere Father Gondrée. They loved the people entrusted to them; they learned the Malagache language, taught catechism in the tongue understood by their flock, and did not hesitate to live as they did without giving a thought to what the other whites would think of them.

The relationship of these two priests with the governor quickly became strained. But unfortunately this was not the only difficulty encountered by the little mission. The unhealthy climate and excessive labors soon brought the first two Fathers to their graves. Two more replaced them, and they too were quickly to succumb. "I do not believe," exclaimed Monsieur Vincent, "there is in our Company a single one who has so little courage as not to go to take the place of those who have died!"

And indeed others went, facing a similar fate if not martyrdom. But what did such sacrifices matter beside the supernatural results these attempts would have? Monsieur Vincent knew better than anyone that, in Tertullian's eternal words, the blood of the sacrificed is always the seed of Christians. At Fort-Dauphin in Madagascar one is still moved to see the tiny church built with their own hands by the first Lazarists. The sturdy missions under the care of Monsieur Vincent's sons in the great island today stand as monuments to these first missionaries.

The Saint's influence

In the history of the world, for those who consider events in the supernatural aspect so well defined by Boussuet, there is what may be called a dialectic of sanctity. The very great saints, the "masthead figures" spoken of by René Grousset, did not appear by chance in time and circumstance; there was a link between their presence and the deep needs of their times.

The message each brought was exactly the one that was awaited. Thus, at the threshold of the first great adventure of spreading the Christian message, St. Paul rose up to signify the Gospel's universality; otherwise Christianity would have remained a small Jewish sect, with limited horizons. In the same way, when chaos was first created by the barbarian invasions, St. Augustine, another saint who was a genius, discerned what was dying in the world and what would survive, and applied Christ's principles to a reconstruction of the world that would not be achieved until six centuries after his death. Also in the same way, St. Benedict prepared future leaders; St. Bernard turned the discipline of the feudal forces into a crusade for spiritual ends; and, at a time when money threatened to dominate the world, the Poor Little Man of Assisi forced recognition of the primacy of poverty.

Such was the role assumed by Monsieur Vincent in his day—to make the West again Catholic after several centuries of decadence, and following the wise and far-seeing warnings of the Council of Trent, to restore to the Church herself and to her priests the authority conferred only by spiritual virtues. And, at a time when all Europe was suffering, was covered with ruins and everywhere threatened with destitution, he tried to restore Christianity to its first great truth, the religion of Love. To all these needs of his time Vincent de Paul responded "plainly and simply" in his own fashion but in such a way that in every domain he acted, although he had followers and equals, he was the first to make the move. Moreover his incredible activities extended to all domains so that everywhere he tilled the field of God.

The exceptional stature of this man was clearly recognized in his day. It is even a proof of the greatness of that "century of spirituality" that it could discern beneath the human features of the former swineherd of the Landes the face of God's authentic witness.

King Louis XIII admired him so much that he wished to have no one else at his bedside when his last hour came; during the last weeks of his life he had such fruitful conversations with him that he had exclaimed: "Ah, Monsieur Vincent, if I am restored to health, I want all the bishops to spend three years with you!" As we have seen, Cardinal de Richelieu had shown him marks of his esteem and at a decisive moment had supported him with all his authority. When she became a widow, Anne of Austria entrusted her spiritual direction to him —and this was not a sinecure since the gracious queen in her forties was not an easy penitent. She made him a sort of minister without portfolio, to direct and put life into everything we now understand as social action; and the influence of the father of the Lazarists over her became such that a young Italian diplomat at the nunciature, named Mazzarini, wrote: "Monsieur Vincent is the channel through which everything comes to Her Majesty's ears."

The Queen even appointed him to her "Council of Conscience," that is to say, to the committee directly under the authority of the throne which discussed the important interests of the Church in France. Particularly did it prepare the list of bishops, since the concordat of 1516 had conceded their nomination to the Crown. Here Monsieur Vincent exerted a considerable influence, working with all his strength to do away with old errors that had proved so damaging to the Church: the

election of children to episcopal sees, the designation of unworthy men. It was a hard battle, and Monsieur Vincent had to face terrible storms, as when he opposed the grant of a benefice to the very young son of the Duc de Rochefoucauld. So uncompromising was his integrity that he was soon on cold terms with the former little *minutante* Mazarin, who had become Cardinal and prime minister of France, and was very close to the heart of the queen. Between the amoral politician and the "clodhopper" in frayed cassock the battle was not equal; nevertheless, when all was said and done, at the end of the combat the result was not the one the artful Italian had hoped to attain.

Over all France, Monsieur Vincent's influence grew constantly, up to the end. The rapid growth of the institutes he founded, the Lazarists and the Daughters of Charity, did not fail to make a deep impression. A new young clergy was emerging from the seminaries created by him. Many priests among those who had followed the Tuesday Conferences or the retreats at Saint-Lazare, or at any rate who had long meditated on the lessons taught by the saint, had become bishops and were spreading his teachings. Among these bishops were Pavillon at Alet, Solminihac at Cahors (later to be beatified), Jacques Raoul and later Dassompierre at Saintes, Sebastian Zamet at Langres, Antoine Godeau at Grasse, Lescot at Chartres, Perrochel at Boulogne, Brandon at Périgueux and, even beyond the borders of France, at Annecy, Juste Guérin.

Due to this admirable constellation of men, a development of pastoral work took place in France that is only now beginning to be recognized, and which explains the Christian qualities of the reign of Louis XIV. Was not the most illustrious exponent of Catholicism a direct disciple of Monsieur Vincent: Jacques-Bénigne Boussuet?

One of Monsieur Vincent's most striking accomplishments was the establishment in Rome of a Lazarist house and the great success it had. Under the direction of one of the congregation's first members, Father Ducoudray, four of St. Vincent's Sons labored throughout the countryside of central Italy. Employing missionary methods later to be revived by Alphonsus Liguori and Paul of the Cross, they also worked in such large cities as Genoa and Turin. This success was even marked by official recognition the importance of which Monsieur Vincent himself underlined: "It has pleased our Holy Father to send ordinands to the poor beggars of the Mission of France. . . ." The Roman clergy coming to the Lazarists to make retreats before ordination—this was indeed a triumph and an unexpected one.

Farther away still, very far from the borders of France, the saint's influence led to the establishment of charities. Maria of Gonzaga, daughter of the Duke of Mantua and Nevers and of Catherine of Lorraine, and the wife in turn of two Polish kings, Ladislas IV and John Casimir, remembering she had been a "Lady of Charity," called the

sons and daughters of Monsieur Vincent to her side. Missions, schools, charitable centers, every aspect of the great Vincentian enterprise, spread to all parts of Poland. Unhappily, the painful military events leading in 1655 to the capture of Warsaw by rebellious Cossacks from the Ukraine and the Swedes, brought an end to these fine undertakings. Lazarists and Gray Sisters, headed by the Mission's leader, Father Ozenne, died in the course of the conflict. But the seed had been sown and a rich harvest was to be reaped later from the fertile soil of Poland.

All this radiation and influence, the example given to his age and received by it, could not fail to be recognized by the Church. In 1729, Monsieur Vincent was beatified; eight years later Clement XII bestowed on him the honors of the altar. And one day Leo XIII was to proclaim him "patron of all works of charity"—a fine title even if it somewhat narrows reference to the fields of action touched by his tireless genius. What glories these were for one who never ceased to require of each of his daughters, of each of his sons, that they live "in the love of his abjection!"

Monsieur Vincent's influence has been confirmed in our own day. He is one of the rare saints —together with St. Louis and Jeanne d'Arc—not passed over in the teaching of French history in French secular schools, as we may see from a number of textbooks. However, we note in none of these manuals the letter addressed to the saint, in 1653, by the aldermen of Rethel telling him that "for two years the region of Champagne, and especially this town, could hardly have kept alive had it not been for your charities." Nor do we find the still more moving letter of the lieutenant-general of Saint-Quentin, thanking him for saving the land from famine and begging him to "be still the father of the nation." "My saint," Voltaire was to exclaim wholeheartedly, "is Vincent de Paul."

It goes without saying that such admiration often arose from "humanitarian" and "philanthropic" sentiments. Rather often in our day the respect inspired by Monsieur Vincent is aroused by similar sentiments, sentiments which to his mind would have been empty of meaning since the only philanthropy that counted for him was that proceeding from the love of God and the charity of Christ.

It is nonetheless true that Monsieur Vincent has remained a popular saint. The film we remarked on earlier as having oversimplified his portrait by stressing his aspect as "an organizer of soup kitchens" has nonetheless helped to bring him and his message alive before a large public. Books have also aided: if the fourteen volumes of *Complete Works* edited by Father Coste are not easily obtainable, there are several volumes of *Selections* permitting us better to acquaint ourselves with the saint's thoughts—those of Father Dodin and Father Chalumeau, for example. And great biographies, such as those of Monsignor Calvet especially, bring before us the lesson of Vincent's life. The anniversary of his death in 1960 was for France the occasion of showing gratitude to a great Frenchman.

The Church owes him even more, and in every manner gave fitting importance to this anniversary. If it be true that great saints—according to a mysterious dialectical law whose other name is Providence—rise up exactly at the moment when their message is needed, it is also true that their message goes far beyond their times. Transcending all history, it places before the Christian soul lessons that cannot be dimmed by the passing of centuries. St. Vincent de Paul, dead three hundred years, remains present among us. The Church of

the centuries that followed and, after these, the Church of our own day, would not be as we know it if the little shepherd of the Landes had not lived, thought, and acted.

Monsieur Vincent is formally present among us in the religious institutes he founded and that continue directly to carry on his vocation. The important place in the Church occupied by the Daughters of Charity we have already noted; the multiple activities of the Lazarists, from missions to the country people in Christian lands to missions beyond the seas, have grown constantly for over three hundred years. Something would be missing in the Christian society of the West if the cornettes of the Daughters of Monsieur Vincent were to vanish from our streets. What traveler on catching

sight of one of them in a strange country, at the other side of the world, does not feel emotion tinged with tenderness and admiration? Anyone who has attended one of the astonishing meetings held in what look like circus tents by one of the groups of Lazarist missionary street preachers called *Forains du Bon Dieu* in de-Christianized country districts or in the "red suburbs" of cities, comes away certain that Monsieur Vincent's message is as alive and actual today as when he carried it to the peasants of Folleville and Châtillon.

Even more deeply has this message infiltrated soil already Catholic and it has brought forth great harvests. It cannot be stressed too strongly that the clergy of France owed in the period that followed, and continue to owe today, the excellence of their formation and adaptation to the Christian task to the spread of the seminaries started by Monsieur Vincent together with Father Olier and St. John Eudes. A direct line can be drawn from them—and the holy Curé of Ars is a mark on the way—down to our times, to Father Chevrier, founder of the Prado, Father Anizan, founder of the Sons of Charity, to Father Lamy of Courneuve and to many, many others whose names are known only to Him who judges all men.

There is scarcely need to point out that in the Church of the twentieth century many of those 96 things which transform Christ's love into action continue to flow from Monsieur Vincent. He

would recognize as his own not only the gentlemen of the "Conferences of St. Vincent de Paul," officially placed under his patronage two hundred years ago, but also the "Little Brothers of the Poor" or the "Good People" who devote themselves to the care of the poorest of the aged, or the Christian men and women who in the immense enterprise of "Catholic Charities" prove that in order to be effective, charity need not be socialized nor narrowed into the framework of so-called "security."

A more living Christianity, constantly worked by the leaven of divine Love; a clergy worthy of its vocation; a more fraternal Church, open to the

humble and disinherited; a deeply humane religious approach, speaking to the heart—all this is
found in the legacy of Monsieur Vincent. Again,
all this is expected and hoped for by believers when
great decisions are to be made; but should we grow
impatient and unmindful of the demand made
upon us as individuals, let us listen to the voice of
Monsieur Vincent raised so imperiously that none
can fail to hear it:

"Do not be content to say: I am a Christian! But
live in such a way that it may be said of you: we
have seen a man who loves God with all his heart
and keeps His Commandments."

Illustrations

1   Contemporary portrait of St. Vincent de Paul at the headquarters of the Priests of the Mission in Paris.

2   Bull of canonization of St. Vincent de Paul signed by Pope Clement XII in 1737.

3   Vincent de Paul in his later years. Picture at the house of the Priests of the Mission at Berceau-de-Saint-Vincent (Landes).

4   House known as the birthplace of St. Vincent, at Ranquine in the vicinity of Pouy—actually a reconstruction.

5   Chapel of Notre Dame de Buzet near Toulouse in which Vincent de Paul celebrated his first Mass.

6   Ex-queen Margaret, first wife of Henry IV of France, at whose court the young Monsieur Vincent served as chaplain. Painting by Rubens in the Louvre.

7   Cardinal de Bérulle, founder of the Oratory and reformer of the clergy, Monsieur Vincent's spiritual director and an important influence in his life.

8   Françoise Marguerite de Silly, wife of Philippe Emmanuel de Gondi, who became an ardent supporter of Monsieur Vincent's charitable activities.

9   Philippe Emmanuel de Gondi, General of the Galleys and Lieutenant-General of the French Army in the Levant. St. Vincent was for a time a tutor in his household.

10   Hospital of Châtillon, meeting-place of Vincent de Paul's first Confraternity of Charity.

11   St. Vincent de Paul, St. François de Sales and St. Jeanne de Chantal in the presence of Queen Anne of Austria. Painting by Jean Restout.

St. Vincent addressing the priests who attended the Tuesday *12* Conferences he instituted for the instruction of the clergy. Among them were Bossuet, the famous orator, and Jean Jacques Olier, founder of the Seminary of St. Sulpice.

Meeting of the Religious Council founded by the Regent, *13* Queen Anne of Austria. From left to right: Cardinal Mazarin, Chancellor Seguer, Queen Anne, the Dauphin Louis XIV, the Grand Penitentiary of Paris, M. Charton, and St. Vincent.

St. Louise de Marillac, co-foundress of the Daughters of *14* Charity. Picture at their motherhouse in the Rue du Bac in Paris.

St. Vincent begging the Ladies of Charity not to abandon the *15* work for the foundlings. St. Louise de Marillac is seen among the ladies of the court assembled to hear his plea.

St. Vincent teaching catechism to the old men and women at *16* the Hospice of the Nom-de-Jésus.

Shrine containing the remains of St. Vincent de Paul in the *17* chapel of the headquarters of the Priests of the Mission, rue de Sèvres, in Paris.

The Very Rev. William M. Slattery, C. M., Superior General, *18* Congregation of the Mission and Daughters of Charity and nineteenth in succession to St. Vincent de Paul.

Simple peasant costume of the first Daughters of Charity. *19*

An example of the dress in common use for a contemporary *20* Daughter of Charity.

Anno Pontiﬁcatus Septimo

✠ Ego Clemens Catholicæ Ecclesiæ Ep̄s

TESTIMONIA TUA DNE ✠ QVAM MIRABILIA
SANCTVS PETRVS · SANCTVS PAVLVS
CLEM ENS
PP. XII

✠ Ego Frater Carolus Ostien. Ep̄s Card. Zuberinus
✠ Ego Petrus Ep̄us Portuens. Card. Otthobonus
✠ Ego Thomas Ep̄us Praeneſtinus Card. Ruﬃus

✠ Ego Ludovicus Ep̄us Albanenſis Card. Belluga
✠ Ego Fabius Ep̄us Tusculanus Card. Aquaviva
✠ Ego Joannes Antonius tit. S. ... quæ in ...

✠ Ego Anno ... tit. S. Francisci Presb. Card.

✠
✠
✠
✠

CLE-
MENS
PAPA
XII

4

5

6

8 9

11

12

14

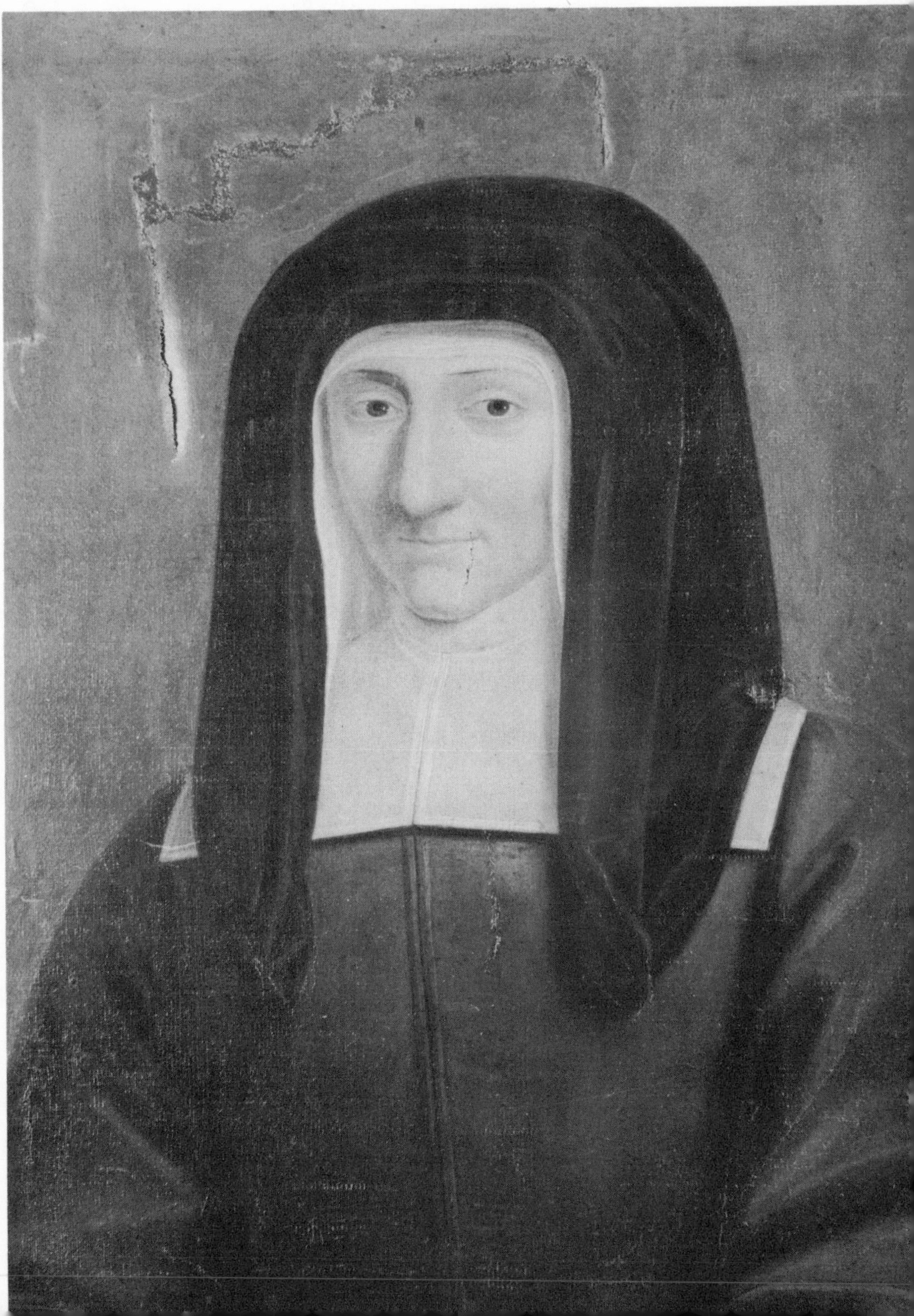

16

18

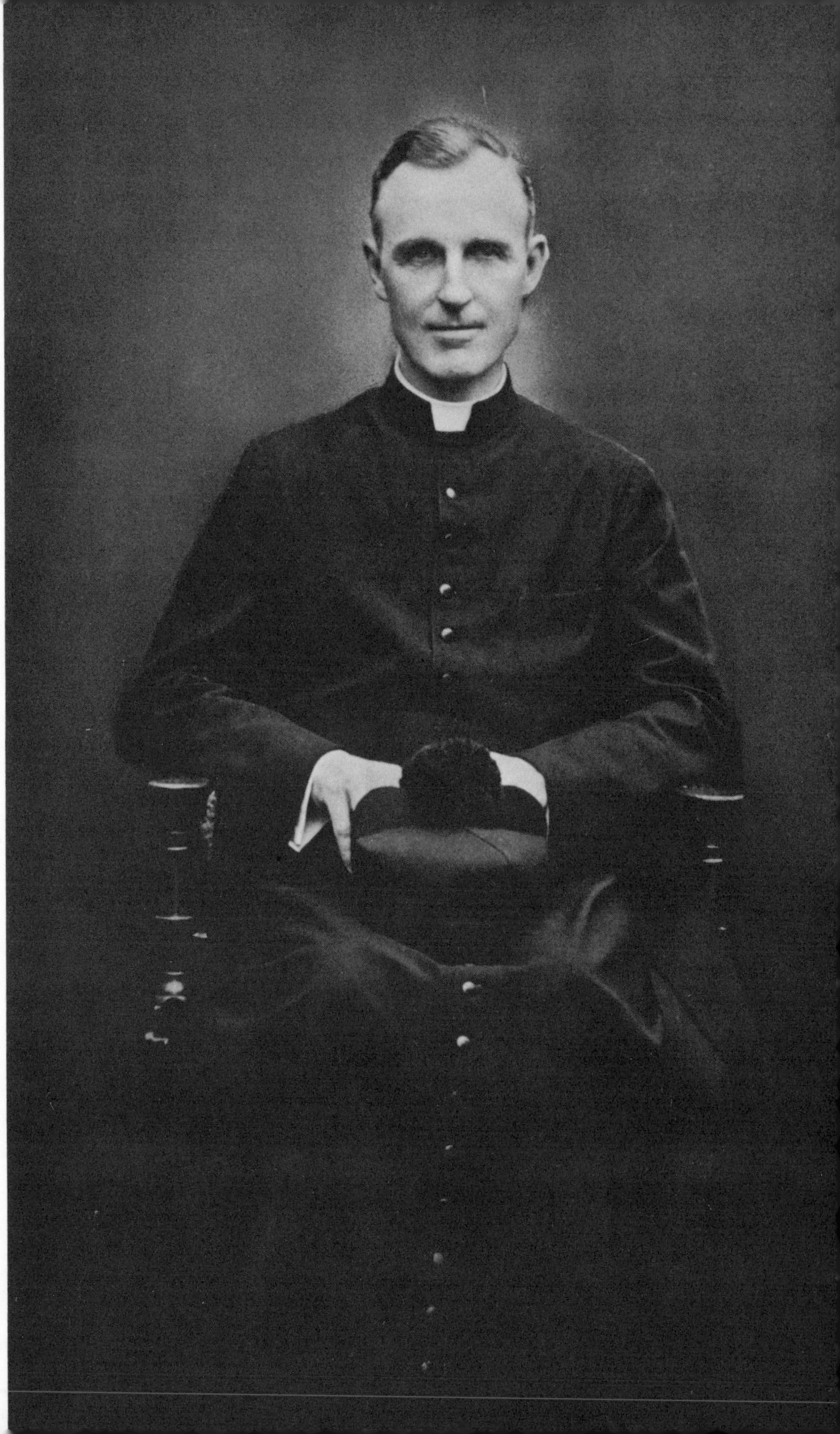

7

Sayings of
Monsieur Vincent

Take care not to spoil God's works by trying to hurry them too much. Take good time and know how to wait.

In God's path

Too often we spoil good works by going too fast, because we are acting according to our own inclinations . . . which make us think what we see to do is practicable and timely. . . . What the good God wishes done is accomplished almost by itself, without our thinking of it. . . .

Over whom would it (Providence) watch if not over its own servants?

Do the good that presents itself to be done. I do not say we should go out indiscriminately and take on everything, but rather those things God lets us know He wants of us. We belong to Him and not to ourselves. If He increases our work, He adds to our strength also.

It is the hour for prayer; if you hear the poor calling you, mortify yourselves and leave God for God, although you must do everything you can not to omit your prayer, for that is what keeps you united to God; and as long as this union lasts you have nothing to fear.

To do one without omitting the other

In serving the poor we are serving Jesus Christ. Oh, my daughters, how true that is! You are serving Jesus Christ in the person of the poor. This is just as true as that you are here before me. A Sister may go to the sick ten times a day, and ten times a day she will find God there.

Our masters the poor

It is quite within reason to serve our masters first. The poor are our masters; they are our kings; we must obey them; and it is no exaggeration to call them this, since Our Lord is in the poor.

Truly, you must serve them but you are even more bound to see to your own salvation.

Wisdom for those under orders

Make your own the precept of always considering that superiors do the best they can; that they can do nothing of importance without reflection and advice; and that it is not permissible . . . to find fault with their behavior. Otherwise there would be as many giving orders as receiving them.

Wisdom for all

You must not expect to live among men, even be they saints, and not to see failings in them; for the condition of this miserable life makes us all subject to these. What then must be done? Certainly, Monsieur, patience and mutual forbearance are the most effectual remedies that Our Lord and experience have taught us for leading others to virtue.

A cure for discontent

To another Brother who stormily demanded to change houses, going so far as to say that, had he to do it over again, he would not have entered the Congregation: Oh, what ill considered words are these! The good God is always the same, now as then, and He deserves to be served now as then. You must not be discouraged because you suffer some aversion, any more than travelers are disheartened by difficulties or sailors by tempests.

One of the principal acts of charity is to bear with our neighbor; and we must realize this undoubted truth, that the difficulties we have with our neighbor spring more from our own poorly mortified tempers than from anything else.

Mea culpa

(Our Lord) can do nothing with our learning nor with our good works if He does not have our hearts. In the name of God, my dear Brother, let us give ourselves to Him; we can do nothing better. Let us become more and more humble; and the better we see our shortcomings, the more will we consider that we have even more than we deserve. I beg His infinite mercy to come down on you and your labors and to make them serve for the sanctification of your soul and the accomplishment of His eternal designs. And do me the charity of applying (their merits) to me also, for I am a great sinner....

Not to be too clever

To a correspondent who spoke of having received extraordinary graces: I praise God for the graces you say you have received from Him, and I pray He will grant you the good use of them.... Those who love God greatly do not boast of it; on the contrary they fear they do not love Him, for to them He is so infinitely lovable that they see their love as nothing in comparison with the love He deserves. However, you praise yours so highly that instead of appearing as great to me as it does to you, your love seems to me very little....

Blessed are the poor in spirit

Perfection does not lie in ecstasies, but in doing well the will of God ... to unite our will with God's so completely that His will and ours are really the same will to do or not to do.

The practice of the presence of God is good indeed, but what is even better, I find, is the practice of doing the will of God in every action; for the one includes the other. Moreover, he who holds himself to the practice of the presence of God may sometimes not be doing the will of God. And tell me, I beg of you, is it not being in the presence of God if one is doing God's will and takes care to form one's intention for that purpose at the beginning of every work and to renew it as one goes along?

Two men have only to live together to put each other to the test, and when you are alone you are a trial to yourself and an object for patience.

You say that a change of house (religious) would deliver you from your troubles; believe me, my brother, it is an error and a snare of the devil to believe this; for we always carry ourselves around with us, together with our imperfections, no matter where we go.

You must remember, Monsieur, there is no superior in the world who does not have to put up with many things from those under his guidance, and that even Our Lord had to suffer much from His own.

To a Daughter of Charity who complained that in church her habit attracted curious and scornful looks: The holy recollection which is fitting in churches will shield you . . . from this inconvenience, especially as you will not see that anyone is looking at you. . . .

We must abandon ourselves to God's Providence and take great care not to run on ahead of it. The works of God achieve themselves and those that are not His soon perish. Rest assured of the truth of a saying that seems paradoxical, that he who hurries delays the things of God.

Oh, what great treasures are hidden in holy Providence and what sovereign honor they render to Our Lord who follow Providence and do not encroach on it!

The good God always takes care of our affairs when we see to His. What happiness . . . to be in the place God has put us, and what unhappiness to set ourselves up there where He has not called us.

It is a want of friendliness to show none at all, to look sad and gloomy, so that you freeze the hearts of those around you. . . . There is another vice at the other extreme of this virtue, which is to be excessively friendly; for instance, to embrace with over-eagerness, to say to one another: "Oh, how I love you. I wouldn't have missed seeing you for anything in the world!" This is excessive friendliness.

To a Brother Helper: I give thanks to God for the charity He has given you and which takes you beyond the seas in desire. . . . It is the means of pleasing God thus to extend your affections in His service. Before Him the will is counted as the deed. . . . Be sure, my dear Brother, He will not allow to go unrewarded the zeal that carries you (in spirit) to Madagascar to help with the salvation of souls and to Genoa to aid our brothers who are afflicted (by the plague). . . . Continue to offer yourself to Him for all parts of the world and all those things in which He sees fit to use you. . . .

Friendliness . . . is the outward effect of charity in the heart. It springs from the heart and shows how very glad you are to be with a particular poor person or Sister. It is the joy you feel when you see a person you love and it shows in your face; for when someone has joy in her heart she cannot hide it; you see it clearly on her face.

Ah, my brother, it is true this is indeed a serious fault. Oh, my brother, shall I say what it was? Oh, Saviour, shall I say what it was? Can I very well mention it without blushing? Brother, I am just as guilty of this as you are, for not having given you sound advice. Can I talk about it? I must swallow my confusion, just as you must, for I am guilty. . . . Oh wretch! It is I, sinner that I am, who am the cause of this. . . . Oh, brother, we must both be covered with shame about this.

Although the King has given grounds for hope of other alms . . . you nevertheless have nothing, for kings promise easily, but they also forget to carry out their promises.

Knowledge of men

Oh, wretch that I am! I have been learning this lesson for a long time (the practice of gentleness) and still I don't know it! I get carried away, I am changeable, I complain, I blame others; for instance, this very evening I scolded the Brother who keeps the door when he came to tell me that someone was asking for me. "For heaven's sake, Brother, what are you doing? I told you not to allow anyone in to speak to me." May God forgive me, and this Brother too! At other times I rebuff this one and that, I speak loudly and cuttingly. I still have not learned to be gentle. I am a wretch! I beg the Company to bear with me and to forgive me.

A man among men

Monsieur, you must empty yourself in order to put on Jesus Christ. You know that ordinary causes produce effects in accordance with their nature: a sheep produces a sheep, a man another man. In the same way if he who rules others . . . is animated by a purely human spirit, those who see him, who listen to him and study to imitate him, will become completely human themselves. . . . On the other hand, if a superior is completely filled with God . . . virtue will proceed from him to edify others, and his every action will be a salutary lesson.

The world awaits saints

Remain cheerful, and in the disposition of desiring all that God wills. And as it is His good pleasure for us always to remain in the holy joy of His love, let us hold to this always in this world so that we may one day have the same joy with Him.

Remain cheerful

Courage! . . . be cheerful and do cheerfully what you have to do. . . . Do all that you can to achieve this, and to be as cheerful as is possible for you.

To François Ducoudray: Is everyone in good humor? Is everyone cheerful?

The way of St. Francis de Sales

When we are at variance with someone, the argument we use enables him to see quite well that we wish to win out; that is why he prepares to resist rather than to recognize the truth. So by beginning in this way, instead of making some kind of opening in his mind, we usually close the door to his heart. On the other hand, how quickly we may open it by gentleness and courtesy.

God's power

Three makes more than ten when Our Lord takes a hand; and this He always does when He has taken away all other means.

No folded arms

The Church is like a great harvest that needs laborers, but laborers who really work!

Courage, let us give ourselves to God once for all. Work! Work!

To preachers: We do not believe a man because he is learned, but because we esteem and love him. The devil is very learned.

134

A certain preacher, superior or confessor trusts too much to his own prudence, his own knowledge and to his own mind. What does God do? He withdraws from him, He leaves him there. And although he works, all he does brings forth no fruit, so in the end he recognizes his uselessness and learns from his own experience that, however talented he may be, without God he can do nothing. *With empty hands*

Let us study in order to have a great, a very great regard for God's majesty and holiness. If the eyes of our soul were strong enough to penetrate even a little to the immensity of His sovereign excellence, oh Jesus! what great emotions would be inspired in us! ... This knowledge we have that God is infinitely above all knowledge and all human understanding should be enough to make us hold Him in infinite respect, to make us annihilate ourselves in His presence, and to speak of His supreme majesty with a great feeling of reverence and submission. And in proportion to our regard for Him will be our love, and this love will create in us an insatiable desire to acknowledge His benefits and to lead true worshippers to Him. *The cornerstone*

To a missionary who returned from preaching: God alone can tell you (of my joy) at the happy success of your sermons. . . . Oh, Monsieur, you have great reason to humble yourself before God and give Him the glory of this, and even to humble yourself before those men who may applaud you. *Paradox*

135

136   Perhaps this grace would not have been granted you had He not removed the obstacles you placed in its way! ... These are the sentiments you should have even if they are not my own; for I am filled with regard for you, and with the hope that the good use to which you put God's blessings will draw down new blessings on you.

Dates of importance
during the life of
St. Vincent de Paul

1572: Massacre of St. Bartholomew.
1581: Montaigne publishes his *Essays*.

1581 (APRIL 24): Birth of Vincent de Paul at Pouy, near Dax.

1591: Birth of St. Louise de Marillac.
1593: Abjuration and consecration of Henry IV.
1594: The Jesuits expelled from France.

1595: Birth of St. Francis Regis.

1595: Vincent a student at college of Dax.
1595–1604: A student at the University of Toulouse.
1600 (SEPTEMBER 23): Ordained a priest at Château-l'Evêque.

1601: Birth of St. John Eudes.
1603: Recall of the Jesuits by Henry IV.

1605–7: Vincent captured by the Turks, a slave at Tunis.
1607–8: Sojourn in Rome.
1608: Vincent's arrival in Paris where he lives at Rue de Sevres.
1609: Chaplain of Queen Margaret.

1608: Francis de Sales' *Introduction to the Devout Life*.

1610: Assassination of Henry IV.

1612 (MAY 2): Installed as curé of Clichy.
1613: Tutor of the Gondis.

1615: Assembly of the clergy to adopt the decrees of the Council of Trent.
1617: Assassination of Concini.

1617: Mission at Folleville; sermon of January 25.
1618 (JANUARY 31): Vincent resigns as curé of Châtillon.
1619 (FEBRUARY 8): Chaplain General of the Galleys.
1622: Appointed superior of Visitation in Paris.
1618–24: Preaches missions on Gondi lands.
1625 (APRIL 17): Foundation of the Congregation of the Mission, at Bons Enfants. (JUNE 23): Death of Madame de Gondi.
1626: Resigns as curé of Clichy.

1618–48: Thirty Years' War.

1619: St. Francis de Sales' visit to Paris.

1622: Death of St. Francis de Sales. Birth of Molière.

1625: Foundation of Port-Royal.

1627: Start of siege of La Rochelle. Birth of Bossuet.

1628 (SEPTEMBER 15): Beginning of Retreats for Ordinands, at Beauvais.
1632: Transfer of Missions to the priory of Saint-Lazare.
1633 (JUNE): Institution of Tuesday Conferences. (NOVEMBER 29): Beginnings of Daughters of Charity.

1633: Second trial of Galileo.

1635: Establishment of French Academy.
1637: Descartes' *Discourse on Method*.
1638: Birth of Louis XIV.

1638: The work for Foundlings.

1639: Birth of Racine.

1640: Publication of the *Augustinus* of Cornelis Jansen.

1643 (APRIL): Death of Louis XIII. Minority of Louis XIV, regency of Anne of Austria. Mazarin prime minister.

1644: Innocent X becomes Pope.

1648–52: The Fronde. Treaty of Westphalia.

1653: Condemnation of the five doctrines of Jansen.

1656: Pascal's *Provinciales*.

1639: M. Vincent at trial of Saint-Cyran. His aid to devastated Lorraine.

1642: Foundation of a major seminary.

1644: Vincent's permanent appointment as Chaplain General of the Galleys. Member of the "Council of Conscience."

1646: Approbation of the Daughters of Charity by archbishop of Paris.

1648: Vincent sends missionaries to Madagascar.

1649 (JANUARY 14): With the Queen at Saint-Germain.

1650: Aid to provinces of Picardy and Champagne.

1651: Sends missionaries and Daughters of Charity to Poland.

1652: Help to the poor of Paris and its environs.

1660 (MARCH 15): Death of Louise de Marillac.

(SEPTEMBER 27): Death of Monsieur Vincent.

The author and his book

HENRI DANIEL-ROPS *is the* nom de plume *of Henri Jules Charles Petiot, born January 19, 1901, in France. The grandson of peasants and the son of an artillery officer, the young student majored simultaneously in law, geography and history, winning the equivalent of a Master's degree in each subject before he was 21 years old. Within a year he was teaching history as an associate professor, which he continued until 1945 when he retired as Professor of History at Neuilly. His* nom de plume *was adopted for his first book, a volume of essays published in 1926. He has used it since for his more than seventy books which include novels, historical studies, poetry, and children's books. His writings have brought him many honors, including election to the Académie Française in 1955, its youngest member. Other honors include Commander of the Order of Saint Gregory the Great, conferred by Pope Pius XII; the Grand Cross conferred by Pope John XXIII; Grand Officer of the Order of Christ; and Officer of the Legion of Honor. He is also winner of the Académie Française' Grand Prix. His greatest successes in this country have been* This is the Mass *and* Jesus and His Times. *Currently he is acting as editor-in-chief of* The Twentieth Century Encyclopedia of Catholicism, *and has contributed one volume to the series as well as supervising the entire 150-volume work. He is a regular contributor to many French magazines and newspapers and edits a popular monthly magazine,* Ecclesia, *as well as publishing an intellectual quarterly. His published works in English are:* Misted Mirror

(*Knopf, 1931*); Two Men in Me (*Rockwell, 1931*); The Poor and Ourselves (*Burns Oates & Washbourne, 1938*); Flaming Sword (*Cassell, 1941*); Death, Where is Thy Victory? (*Cassell, 1946*); Sacred History (*Longmans, Green, 1949*); Where Angels Pass (*Cassell, 1950*); St. Paul: Apostle of Nations (*Fides, 1953*); Jesus and His Times (*Dutton, 1954*); Book of Books (*Kenedy, 1956*); Cathedral and Crusade (*Dutton, 1957*); This Is the Mass (*Hawthorn, 1958*); What Is the Bible? (*part of* The Twentieth Century Encyclopedia of Catholicism), (*Hawthorn, 1958*); The Heroes of God (*Hawthorn, 1959*); The Book of Mary (*Hawthorn, 1960*) *and* Golden Legend of Young Saints (*Kenedy, 1960*).

MONSIEUR VINCENT (*Hawthorn, 1961*) *was designed by Ernst Reichl after the French edition of René Perrin. The body type is Granjon, designed for Linotype under the supervision of George W. Jones and named after the French type designer, Robert Granjon. Type was set by the Atlantic Linotype Co., Inc., Brooklyn, N.Y. The text and illustrations were printed by lithography by The Murray Printing Co., Forge Village, Massachusetts. The book was bound by the Montauk Book Manufacturing Co., Inc., New York City.*

A HAWTHORN BOOK